Teaching Adults
A Literacy Resource Book

developed by
ProLiteracy

New Readers Press

ISBN 978-1-56420-039-6

Copyright © 2003, 1994
New Readers Press
Division of ProLiteracy
1320 Jamesville Avenue, Syracuse, New York 13210
www.newreaderspress.com

Printed in the United States of America
19   18   17   16   15

All proceeds from the sale of New Readers Press materials
support literacy programs in the United States and worldwide.

Illustrated by Cheri Bladholm
Diagrams by Rich Harrington

Contents

Introduction

The United States faces an alarming literacy problem. Although estimates vary, most major surveys say that at least 20 million adult Americans cannot read and write well enough to function effectively in their daily lives. Thousands of volunteer tutors, professional educators, and adult new readers themselves are working to change this situation.

This Book

Teaching Adults: A Literacy Resource Book is designed to provide tutors and teachers with tools to meet the diverse needs of learners. It pulls together many of the "best practice" ideas in the field of adult literacy. The book is also a companion piece to the *Training by Design* literacy tutor training materials. It includes background information on literacy, as well as 69 specific activities that tutors can use with literacy learners.

Many people shared in preparing this book. It also builds on the work done by literacy practitioners across the country. Pat Bleakley, Linda Church, Margaret Hampstead, Jane Hugo, and Wendy Stein worked on the research and writing. Dr. Betty Aderman shared her library and her reading expertise. Jane MacKillop and Lydia Wallace provided particular help with the sections on development and assessment of portfolios. Twyla Ferguson, Dr. Alton Greenfield, Barbara Burks Hanley, Lorraine Loitz, and Dr. Mary Dunn Siedow gave helpful comments as content reviewers. Velma Carlson provided much needed and timely word processing assistance. Many New Readers Press staff members helped pull the project together and were responsible for creating a resource that is both easy to read and visually attractive.

Tutoring Philosophy

The material in this book expresses ProLiteracy America's commitment to the following beliefs:

Each Adult Learner Is a Unique Individual

Adult learners bring a wealth of knowledge and experience to the learning process. Each adult learner is a unique individual with his or her own needs and interests. This idea is at the core of teaching adults. In order to ensure success, the tutor or teacher must work with the learner to tailor the program to the learner's long-term goals and short-term objectives.

Tutoring Is Effective

Traditional instructional methods failed many of the adults in literacy programs. Tutoring, whether in small groups or one-to-one, offers another chance. Tutors can develop a respectful and encouraging relationship with learners and create a new environment for learning. In this new environment, tutors, trained in basic instructional techniques and learning theory, can guide and support a learner's literacy development.

Reading and Writing Are Meaning-based Processes

The goal of literacy instruction is to help learners gain the skills, knowledge, and attitudes needed to actively make meaning out of written language—to see themselves as capable readers and writers.

To make meaning, people must be able to do the following:

- recognize the language forms (e.g., letters, words, style, and formats) being used in what they read and use these forms in what they write

- understand the author's purpose for writing and have a purpose for what they themselves write

- react to what they read using their prior knowledge about the topic, their experience, and their values and expect others to do the same with what they write

- apply the meanings they make to their lives

A Variety of Instructional Approaches Is Needed

Literacy teacher Marilyn Gillespie tells us, "Literacy is the 'exercised' ability to use reading and writing to get information one needs and to exchange it with others. This implies that learners must connect literacy to its meaning in their everyday lives and find ways to determine for themselves the conditions under which they will use reading and writing. It means there is not just one literacy, decided on by experts, but 'many literacies,' defined by each of us, individually and together" (Marilyn Gillespie, *Many Literacies: Modules for Training Adult Beginning Readers and Tutors,* Amherst, MA: Center for International Education, 1990, p. 2). No one instructional approach or published series can address all the ways different adults will need to use their literacy skills. Consequently, tutors need to be able to use a variety of teaching techniques and materials. They need to understand the following concepts:

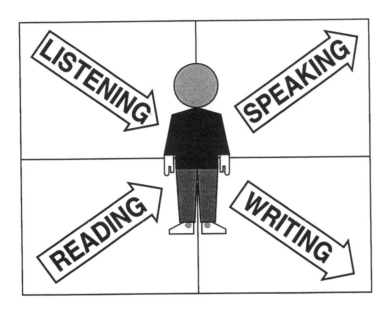

- Listening, speaking, reading, and writing are interrelated parts of a person's language acquisition process. Instruction in reading and writing should allow learners to integrate all four of these communication tools and to become active, flexible, and independent communicators of ideas and feelings.

- Literacy instruction should help learners to participate in their communities and families and to use their skills to improve the world in which they live.

- Literacy instruction should take into account the personal feelings, needs, and concerns of learners. It should aim to overcome any sense of past failure, to encourage risk taking, and to enable learners to reach specific goals.

- Literacy instruction should flow from learner assessment. Assessment should be a shared and ongoing process that helps ensure that learning programs meet learners' goals and objectives.

- Literacy instruction will be more effective if learners help identify objectives and specific activities, are guided by the tutors during the activities, and reflect on the learning afterward. This process enables learners to tie instruction to their needs, experience success during instruction, and recognize what progress they have made.

What Is ProLiteracy?

ProLiteracy is a nonprofit, 501(c)(3) educational corporation. Its mission is to sponsor educational programs and services designed to "empower adults and their families by assisting them to acquire the literacy practices and skills they need to function more effectively in their daily lives and participate in the transformation of their societies." ProLiteracy provides these programs and services through:

- **U.S. Programs**
- **International Programs**
- **New Readers Press**

The purpose of **U.S. Programs** is to advocate for the needs of adult learners and to provide support to the organizations and agencies that serve them. Examples of this support include the following:

- specialized information provided through print, e-mail, and the organization's Web site;
- technical assistance and training;
- an annual conference with a broad range of training opportunities
- an individual and group affiliation program with specific benefits for each category of affiliates;
- an accreditation system for local literacy programs;
- a certification system for trainers who conduct staff development workshops for instructions and volunteer tutors; and
- involvement of local programs in the planning and field-testing of materials, such as *Teaching Adults: A Literacy Resource Book,* to ensure that the products are effective in meeting local needs.

New Readers Press (NRP), is an award-winning publisher that works with authors, educators, and top-name consultants to develop instructional materials and resources for instructors and volunteer tutors. NRP distributes approximately 450 titles,

International Programs works with 82 international partner organizations that provide literacy programs in 47 developing countries in Asia, Africa, Latin America, and the Middle East. These organizations are staffed by citizens of the countries in which they are located. They receive training and technical assistance from ProLiteracy staff as well as small grants to support their work. International Programs utilizes a "Literacy Solutions" process, which allows learners to develop native-language literacy skills while at the same time acquiring information they need to solve problems unique to their communities (nutrition, health, safe drinking water, transportation, employment, etc.)

New Readers Press (NRP) is an award-winning publisher that works with authors, educators, and top-name consultants to develop instructional materials and resources for instructors and volunteer tutors. NRP distributes approximately 450 titles, including selected products from other publishers. One of NRP's most widely-read publications is its weekly newspaper for adult new readers: *News for You*. (See Appendix A for a list of some of the other NRP products.)

- Contacts:
  ProLiteracy
  1320 Jamesville Avenue
  Syracuse, NY 13210-4241
  (315) 422-9121
  info@proliteracy.org
  www.proliteracy.org

  New Readers Press
  1320 Jamesville Avenue
  Syracuse, NY 13210-4241
  (800) 448-8878
  www.newreaderspress.com

ProLiteracy was created in 2002 through the merger of Laubach Literacy International and Literacy Volunteers of America, Inc.

Becoming a Nation of Readers and Writers

What Is Literacy?

At one time, literate people were those who could sign their names and recognize simple words. In today's complex society, daily life demands a much higher level of reading and writing. A modern definition of literacy must acknowledge these increased demands. It must also treat literacy as a tool —a means to an end—rather than the end itself.

The National Adult Literacy Survey of 1993 (described on p. 14) defined literacy this way: "Using printed and written information to function in society, to achieve one's goals, and to develop one's knowledge and potential." This definition does not tie literacy to one standard ability or grade level, but recognizes that literacy is related to the needs of each individual.

The Problem in the United States

Over the years, there have been many different definitions of literacy. Therefore, estimates of the extent of illiteracy in the United States differ. The following are some of the major studies that have attempted to measure adult illiteracy in this country:

- 1975: The federally funded Adult Performance Level Study (APL), done by the University of Texas, surveyed 7,500 adults to measure their ability to apply skills in the fields of occupational knowledge, consumer economics, community resources, health, and government and law. Researchers estimated that 20% of the adults were functionally illiterate, 34% were marginally literate ("just getting by"), and 46% were fully literate ("proficient"). If these rates were applied to the 1980 Census figures, it would indicate that 30 million adults were functionally illiterate and 50 million were marginally literate in the United States in 1980.

- 1982: The English Language Proficiency Study (ELPS), conducted by the U.S. Census Bureau, required 3,400 adults (20 years old and older) to select the word or phrase that best defined each of 26 examples of language typical of government forms. The standard of literacy was set at 20 correct answers. Thirteen percent of the sample group failed to meet this standard. If this result were applied to the 1980 Census figures, it would indicate that 17 to 21 million American adults were illiterate.

- 1985: The National Assessment of Educational Progress (NAEP), done by the Educational Testing Service, surveyed the literacy skills of 3,600 adults ages 21 to 25. The survey checked three types of literacy skills: prose, document, and quantitative. It found that an overwhelming majority of young adults performed adequately at the lower level of each type. However, only a relatively small percentage performed the more difficult tasks associated with each type.

- 1993: The U.S. Department of Education released the results of its National Adult Literacy Survey, administered by the Educational Testing Service. More than 26,000 adults (16 years old or older) were asked to complete typical everyday tasks that require prose, document, or quantitative literacy.

  Between 46% and 51% of the participants had difficulty with tasks that required higher-level reading and problem-solving skills. These people were far less likely to be employed full time, to earn high wages, and to vote than those who performed better. They were far more likely to be receiving food stamps and living in poverty.

  These results indicate that some 90 million adults in the United States may have inadequate literacy skills.

Other indicators of a serious literacy gap include the following:

- Approximately 16.5 million adults over 25 have less than a ninth-grade education. An additional 22.8 million adults over 25 attended high school but did not earn a high school diploma (1990 U.S. Census).

- About 34.8% of women who are heads of households do not have a high school diploma (Department of Labor).

- In 1991, about 3.9 million Americans between the ages of 16 and 24 (12.5%) had not completed high school and were not currently enrolled in school ("Dropout Rates in the United States: 1991," U.S. Department of Education).

- Forty percent of all current jobs require limited skills, but only 27% of newly created jobs fall into low skill categories (U.S. Department of Labor, *Workforce 2000: Work and Workers for the 21st Century,* 1987).

Building Literacy Strength

At an education summit meeting in 1989, the nation's governors set this goal: "By the year 2000, every adult American will be literate and will possess the knowledge and skills necessary to compete in a global economy and exercise the rights and responsibilities of citizenship." Literacy tutors, teachers, and learners across the country are working in community centers, schools, workplaces, churches, family literacy programs, prisons, libraries, and homeless shelters to make this goal a reality.

New Readers Speak Out

Every person has his or her own reasons for wanting to learn to read and write. Here, two new readers express what learning means to them. These stories were included in *Not by Myself . . . ,* a collection of stories by new writers from the southeastern United States, published by Literacy South.

Reading Helps Me Reach for the Stars

by Maybelle Biggerstaff

How did it all come about for me? When my stepdaughter was in kindergarten, it hit me like a ton of bricks. "Oh, no!" I thought to myself. I can't read or write very well. What am I going to do when she gets into the higher grades and asks me to help her with her homework? Of course, that day came. Like all illiterate people we have ways to get around any situation. I would tell her your daddy can help you with that. He's better at spelling, and math, than I am. Well I got around that one I thought.

Being illiterate stayed on my mind a lot. I just didn't know where to go to get help. I wouldn't tell my husband, because he had no idea. He always thought I just dropped out of High School. He never asked what grade I dropped out of so it was never talked about.

One day I decided to stop by the library on the way home from work. Walking up to the desk where the librarian was standing, I asked her "if they had a program to help people who can't read." The librarian gave me a phone number to call. Of course I called it, and what did I get but an answering machine, which at that time I wouldn't talk on. I just hung up.

Shortly after that I was at work and some of the girls were talking about going back to night school to get their GED. They said, "Why don't you go back to school with us?" I thought I would die, for I couldn't let them know that GED wasn't what I needed. So I decided maybe if I studied hard enough I could do it anyway. So I gave it a good try. I would stay up half the night trying to do my books, going to bed at 2:00 a.m. and getting up at 5:00 a.m. to go to work. I was also trying to visit my mother three days a week, which was in a nursing home. Going to school two nights a week, doing all my housework, it didn't take long before I was burned out. My husband told me I had to quit school, so I did.

One day I was home alone, I decided to watch T.V. awhile. I turned it on and there I was watching a story about a man who couldn't read or write. As I watched the story I saw myself. The trouble he was having and things he was going through was like me. At the end of the story they put a number on the T.V. screen. I wrote it on a piece of paper. Later when I was by myself, I called it. A lady named Nancy talked with me on the phone, and set up an appointment, for me to come and see her. Nancy told me how to get there, and where I had to go. When I got there I was scared to death, my hands were shaking, and my knees were knocking. After I talked to Nancy awhile, I wasn't scared anymore. She took down the information she needed. She told me they would call me when they found me a tutor.

My goals in life now are so different than they were two years ago. Now I can use a dictionary and read a road map, balance a check book and even write checks out and spell the numbers right. I can read a newspaper and use the phone book to look up phone numbers. But most of all I like reading because I can read a book and understand it.

I love reading very much. Now my goal is to get my GED, become a Veterinary Assistant. Most of all I want to tell people who can't read or write, there is a rainbow. Reading to me is like finding the pot of goal at the end of the rainbow.

Not Being Able to Read

by "The Bird"

I will always be scared of someone finding out I cannot read. I do not understand people today or in high school. When I was in high school I went from class to class and grade to grade not being able to read. Do you think the teachers knew or cared that I could not read? I don't believe they cared; if they did, why didn't they say something.

Today I can read better and I enjoy reading. Sometimes I get so frustrated when I cannot read or spell something. It's that one word that gets me. I am a quiet person and I think it is because of the way I read. Today reading is a big part of my life. If people know you can't read well or at all they will call you dumb.

I looked for two years for someone to teach me to read. I did not ask for help reading in school because I was afraid people would call me dumb or worthless. My tutor is a wonderful teacher to work with me week in and week out. I am thankful for her, and I will never forget her. I like going to class, but I know one day it will end.

I hope one day the frustration will be gone, but I will not give up. This quiet person lives on. I hope one day someone will understand what I'm saying about reading.

What is it like to read or spell something without getting frustrated? Maybe one day I will know.

Stories on pp. 15–17 are from *Not By Myself* . . . , Literacy South, 1992. Used by permission.

Thinking about Adults as Learners

Literacy volunteers teach people, not books or skills. When you teach adults, you need to consider the following:

- characteristics and needs of adult learners in general and new readers in particular
- special needs
- individual learning styles

General Characteristics and Needs of Adult Learners

Learning as an adult is different in many ways from learning as a child. To be an effective tutor or teacher, you'll need to understand what adults are like and what they need and want in a learning situation. The chart below sums up some important characteristics of adult learners (not just new readers) and the implications for teaching:

Adult learners	As a tutor or teacher, you should
want and deserve respect	give frequent praise and support
	emphasize the skills and strengths the learner already has
	design lessons so that the learner experiences success
	believe in the learner and his or her ability to learn
	treat tutoring as a partnership between equals
	use the learner's first name only if you invite the learner to use your first name and he or she is comfortable doing so

Adult learners	As a tutor or teacher, you should
are used to making decisions	involve the learner in setting goals and objectives
	offer choices of activities and materials
	ask the learner to evaluate the lessons
	respect the learner's priorities and opinions
are busy people	develop lesson plans that address priority needs
	use the tutoring time carefully
	be flexible in assigning homework
	help the learner schedule homework time
have to deal with emergencies and unexpected situations	make an agreement to call if either you or the learner cannot make it to a session
	have alternative activities ready in case the learner did not have time to prepare
have a wealth of life experience	build self-esteem by emphasizing how much the learner already knows or can do
	be open to what the learner can teach you
	design instructional activities around the learner's work, community, family, politics, hobbies, friends, or current interests
sometimes feel insecure about using new skills on their own	provide plenty of opportunities to practice new skills
	practice an exercise with the learner before asking the learner to do it alone or for homework
	provide support, such as audiotapes of a reading assignment
	encourage the learner to use computer programs (where available) to reinforce skills
	emphasize the learner's progress
	don't ask something you know the learner doesn't know
have their own values and beliefs	respect the learner's values and don't try to change them
	don't judge

Adult learners	As a tutor or teacher, you should
may have special physical needs	be sensitive to possible sight or hearing problems
	provide adequate lighting
	speak clearly
	meet in a place that is comfortable and accessible to the learner
	provide adequate break time
want to apply what they learn to their present lives	find out what the learner's needs are
	show how a skill or lesson helps the learner move closer to meeting those needs

Characteristics of Adult New Readers

Adult new readers share the characteristics of all adult learners. Adult new readers might also have some of the needs or characteristics listed in the chart below.

Adult new readers	As a tutor or teacher, you should
may fear school	find out what school experiences were unpleasant for the learner and avoid re-creating them
	stress what the learner has done right
	avoid criticizing or ridiculing the learner
	sit next to, rather than stand over, the learner
	de-emphasize formal testing
may have problems meeting basic needs because of unemployment or poverty	refer the learner to an appropriate source of assistance if the learner wants help
may find planning for the future difficult	help the learner set goals for reading and writing
	be prepared to develop supplemental lessons that speak to special needs or interests, such as how to obtain job training or write a résumé

Adult new readers	As a tutor or teacher, you should
may be embarrassed or ashamed about being unable to read and write	reassure the learner that many adults are in the same situation
	encourage the learner to attend a student support group, if your program has one
	be supportive and let the learner know there is nothing wrong with him or her
	find a private place for lessons if the learner is uncomfortable working in a public area

Special Needs

Hearing and Vision Problems

Older people often begin to experience problems with sight or hearing. In addition, many adult new readers do not have access to regular health care and may have problems that have never been diagnosed. Others may not be able to afford new glasses or other services they need. Below are signs that you should look for and suggestions for what you can do.

Hearing problems

The learner may tell you that he or she has a hearing problem, or you may discover it through observation. Notice if the learner talks loudly, often asks you to repeat yourself, misunderstands you, or turns an ear toward you when you speak.

If these things happen, you can

- enunciate clearly

- speak loudly without yelling

- make sure the learner is looking at you when you start to speak

- ask the learner to repeat explanations or instructions so you can check understanding

- recommend that the learner have a hearing check

Keep in mind that some learners may have had hearing problems since early childhood. Such problems may have affected their ability to develop and use language effectively. As a result, they may also have had problems learning to read.

Vision problems

Signs of vision problems include squinting, holding a book very close or very far away, bending low over the table, headaches, eye fatigue, inability to read small print, and misreading words. If you suspect vision problems, you can

- ask the learner to tell you if the print is too small

- work in a well-lighted area

- use large-print books or enlarge the text by using a photocopy machine

- use a magnifying bar

- recommend that the learner have an eye exam

- find out if a group in your area (such as the Lions Club) can help provide glasses for people who can't afford them

Some people with 20/20 vision have other kinds of vision problems that can interfere with learning to read. For example, a person might have difficulty with binocular vision (using both eyes together). Dr. Dale Jordan, a learning disabilities specialist from Oklahoma City, suggests that tutors and teachers observe the learner for the following signs. They may indicate other vision problems. (This information was presented at the Arkansas Literacy Conference, April 1991.)

- holds the pencil in a "funny" way (if right-handed)

- puts his or her head on the desk to read

- slumps in the chair

- closes one eye

- develops a headache after only a few minutes of reading

- complains of tired eyes

- confuses right and left

- has difficulty looking steadily at the work

- fidgets

- has eyes that water

- yawns a lot

- skips or reverses words or letters

Learning Disabilities

Not everyone who has problems learning to read has learning disabilities. However, researchers suggest that between 30% and 80% of adults in literacy programs display characteristics typical of individuals with learning disabilities. The term *learning disabilities* refers to a broad spectrum of processing disorders that arise from problems in taking in, storing, retrieving, or expressing information.

The Learning Disabilities Association of America describes learning disabilities as follows: "Specific learning disabilities is [*sic*] a chronic condition of presumed neurological origin which selectively interferes with the development, integration, and/or demonstration of verbal and/or nonverbal abilities. Specific learning disabilities exists [*sic*] as a distinct handicapping condition which varies in its manifestations and in degree of severity. Throughout life the condition can affect self-esteem, education, vocation, socialization, and/or daily living activities." (*A Learning Disabilities Digest for Literacy Providers*, Learning Disabilities Association of America, 1991.)

Research and experience have shown that learning disabilities are not related to mental retardation. Learning disabilities rather reflect a discrepancy between a person's ability and performance levels. The person usually has at least average intelligence. The measurement of ability and performance can be particularly frustrating for a teacher because results are often inconsistent. The learner may demonstrate high to very high aptitude and achievement in one area; in another area, results may indicate below average to very low achievement. In literacy programs, adults with learning disabilities may exhibit a wide range of proficiency levels.

People with learning disabilities can learn to cope with these difficulties. They need to understand that their learning problems are caused by specific conditions that can be identified and addressed.

Tutors, in consultation with their literacy programs, must determine whether problems that occur in tutoring are caused by the methods of instruction or learning disabilities. LLA recommends that tutors contact their program if they suspect a learner has learning disabilities. The program should seek professional help to assess the individual.

The following behaviors may indicate learning disabilities if they continue over a long period of time:

- hyperactivity (e.g., restlessness, poor motor coordination, talking a lot but frequently with incomplete thoughts)

- hypoactivity (e.g., reacting slowly, working slowly, seeming unemotional)

- attention problems (e.g., daydreaming, seeming confused, having difficulty concentrating, being easily distracted)

- impulsivity (e.g., acting without thinking and without concern for consequences, not staying with a task, saying one thing and meaning another, speaking at inappropriate times)

- other general behaviors (e.g., misinterpreting what others say; having memory problems; being clumsy; displaying poor decision-making skills; having difficulty managing time; displaying poor fine motor skills; confusing left and right, up and down, or east and west)

If you know you are working with a learning-disabled adult, try a variety of techniques to build on the learner's strengths and compensate for weaknesses. In addition to using multisensory techniques (discussed under "Individual Learning Styles" later in this chapter), consider some of the following suggestions. If you're not sure which will work best with a specific learner, ask your literacy program for assistance. The most important thing is to keep trying. Learning may be slower and more frustrating for someone with learning disabilities, but the results can be well worth the extra effort required.

- Present information in small, manageable steps.

- Structure activities.

- Provide frequent reinforcement.

- Provide frequent feedback.

- Teach new material in concrete ways. Give examples.

- Relate new material to the learner's everyday life.

- Discuss and study new vocabulary words before they appear in the instructional material.

- Experiment with large print.

- Use graph paper to help with letter spacing in writing.

- Prepare the learner for changes in routine.

- Rephrase questions during discussions and on assessments.

- Make frequent eye contact. (This may be very difficult for some disabled learners.)

- Set up instructional space away from distractions (e.g., doors, windows, and heating and air conditioning units).

- Restate information in a variety of ways.

- Use a colored transparency to change the contrast between ink and paper on reading materials.

- Teach and encourage the use of mnemonics (techniques for memorizing information).

- Be well prepared for each session.

- Use untimed tests.

- Use multiple choice tests.

(The information in this section was taken from *A Learning Disabilities Digest for Literacy Providers,* Learning Disabilities Association of America, 1991.)

Individual Learning Styles

A learning style is the way a person takes in, stores, and retrieves information. People differ in which of the five physical senses (hearing, sight, touch, taste, and smell) they depend on when learning and what kind of environment helps them learn best.

The Physical Senses: Pathways to the Brain

The three main senses a learner uses are sight, hearing, and touch. A learner can be described by which sense he or she relies on most. (See chart below.)

Type of Learner	Sense Relied On	Characteristics
auditory	hearing	learns by listening and discussing
visual	sight	learns by visualizing and by looking at text, charts, pictures, etc.
kinesthetic/tactile	movement, touch	learns by doing and being physically involved in a task

Each of these senses provides a different pathway for information to reach a person's brain.

Some people are very strong in one pathway, while others may use two or even three pathways well. A multisensory approach to teaching and learning involves all three of these senses. It has the following advantages:

- It ensures that the tutor will provide opportunities for a learner to use the sense that works best, even if the tutor is not sure what that sense is.

- The more pathways a learner uses, the more likely he or she is to retain the information.

- People tend to rely on different senses depending on the tasks at hand.

The chart on p. 26 outlines some learning style characteristics and ideas for involving each of the three senses in your teaching.

Auditory learners	As a tutor or teacher, you can
process most easily information they hear	read to the learner
prefer oral instructions	make audiotapes of reading selections for the learner to use while reading
understand information best when they repeat it aloud after hearing it	encourage the learner to discuss or summarize a reading passage
can discriminate between words that sound alike (*bet/bat*) and between similar sounds (*s/z*)	ask the learner to repeat instructions
	use oral reading techniques (see Activities #16–19)
can reproduce information they hear: sounds, words, grammatical structures	use music and rhythms to reinforce learning

Visual learners	As a tutor or teacher, you can
"see" information in their minds (They form mental pictures.)	choose materials with pictures and other illustrations
	use flash cards, diagrams, and charts
prefer written instructions or demonstrations	use language experience activities to help the learner see his or her words and ideas in print (see Activities #12–15)
	write instructions to reinforce oral instructions
	use a highlighter to call attention to key words or phrases
	use visualization techniques to help with spelling, sight words, and comprehension

Kinesthetic/tactile learners	As a tutor or teacher, you can
are physically active	have the learner trace letters or words (when learning to spell)
learn by touching and doing	
may recall information more easily when some physical action is involved: walking, touching objects, movement, taking notes	develop writing activities to reinforce the reading skills being learned
	ask the learner to draw a picture that represents the story
would rather do something than talk or write about it	use letter cards or letter game tiles to spell words
	use word cards to form sentences
	use computers or simulation and board games
	provide frequent breaks during sessions
	change activities often

Teaching Adults: A Literacy Resource Book

The Environment

Environmental factors can also influence how effectively people learn. Take the following factors into account as you and the adult learner consider when and where to schedule your sessions and what in your learning space is helpful or distracting.

Time of day

Some people learn better in the morning, others in the afternoon, and still others in the evening.

Setting

Some people have difficulty concentrating in their homes because there are too many distractions. Some are uncomfortable working in public areas. Some prefer a particular type of chair or a particular table height.

Length of session

Some people like to work in long uninterrupted sessions; others prefer short sessions and frequent breaks.

Involvement with others

Some people learn best alone; others prefer to work in groups.

Level of organization

Some people need their work space to be very organized and neat. Others don't mind—and actually seem to prefer—a certain amount of clutter.

Noise

Some people like noise or music in the background while they work. Others require total silence.

Lighting

People have different needs. Some need bright lights; others prefer dimmer lighting. Some disabled readers have problems with fluorescent lighting but work well in natural light.

Temperature

Some people have difficulty concentrating if the room is too cold or too hot.

You probably can't control everything about the environment in which you tutor. However, you can try to be aware of the needs of the learner. You might also discuss these needs with the learner. Then the learner can consider them when planning where to study or do homework.

Finding a Starting Point

The initial learner assessment helps you to

- identify the learner's goals and needs, the abilities the learner already has, and the abilities he or she needs to develop

- plan instruction and identify teaching methods and materials most appropriate for the learner

- have a baseline that can be used later to measure learner progress and ability to use literacy to meet personal needs (Suggestions for using assessment to measure a learner's progress during tutoring are discussed on pp. 128–133.)

Types of Initial Learner Assessment

There are four general types of initial assessment. Some literacy programs use a combination of types to meet different needs.

Standardized Tests

These tests are most like the standardized tests given in schools. They usually give results in terms of approximate grade level equivalents. These results may not take into account an adult's knowledge and experience.

This statement illustrates the focus of standardized tests: "I can read and write as well as the average student in grade _____."

Competency-based Assessment

This kind of assessment measures a person's ability to apply basic skills in functional contexts, such as reading calendars, maps, traffic signs, and newspaper ads.

Competency-based assessment is best summed up with this sentence: "I am able to use my reading and writing skills to perform the following functional tasks: _____."

Materials-based Assessment

This form of testing helps determine where to place a learner in a specific set of instructional materials. It is rarely applicable to other materials.

This statement illustrates the focus of materials-based assessments: "I have mastered the skills taught in the following materials: _____."

Performance Assessment

This form of assessment focuses on why the learner came to the program, what the learner wants to do with reading and writing, and how the learner currently uses these tools in his or her own life. Performance assessment involves the learner in self-assessment. It helps the tutor understand what the learner thinks about reading and writing and about being a learner. It involves the learner in a range of reading and writing activities that can help expand his or her personal definition of literacy.

Performance assessment is summed up with this sentence: "I have used reading and writing in the following ways: _____."

Doing Your Own Assessment

Some literacy programs may conduct an intake interview, do the initial learner assessment, and pass the information on to the tutor. In other programs, the tutor may need to do the assessment.

Activities #1–5, below, will help you learn more about the learner you will work with and be better able to design lessons to fit the learner's special needs.

The ideas are similar to those in *Whole Language for Adults,* published by New Readers Press (see Appendix A), which uses performance assessment. You can also use many of these activities even if you use one of the other types of assessment described above.

As you and the learner work through the assessment, you can make notes on a form like the one on pp. 35–37. You may want to adapt the form and the activities to your own needs or program requirements. Both your observations and those of the learner are important in this process.

Activities #1–5 will help you work with a learner to explore the following five areas:

- background information (what experience, responsibilities, and involvements the learner brings)

- current reading and writing (what the learner thinks about reading and writing; how the learner uses reading and writing now)

- reading and writing needs (what the learner wants to be able to do)

- abilities needed (what the learner needs to know in order to meet those needs)

- feelings about the assessment process

Don't try to cover all five areas in your first lesson. Gather the information informally during the first few meetings, giving the learner opportunities to demonstrate reading and writing abilities.

As you make your initial assessment, note any feelings or observations that the learner makes about his or her strengths and weaknesses.

Activity 1 Background Information

Find out about these general areas:

- the learner—full name; address; phone numbers; best way to contact; age; physical needs related to hearing, sight, or mobility

- the learner's household—names and ages of children or grandchildren he or she is responsible for, other adults in the home

- work—what the learner does now, name and address of employer, kinds of work the learner has done in the past

- interests and hobbies—spare-time activities and what the learner likes about them

- learning experiences as a child and teenager—where the learner went to school, what school was like for him or her, last grade completed

- learning experiences as an adult—classes in reading and writing, other kinds of classes (trade or technical, in the military, etc.), things the learner can do well and how he or she learned them, best learning experiences as an adult and what made them good, adult learning experiences the learner liked least and why

Suggestion

You can list the things you'd like to know and then create a language experience story as the learner talks about them. (See Activity #8.)

Activity 2 Current Reading and Writing

Ask the learner

- what the learner thinks makes someone a good reader or writer

- what the learner reads and writes now at home or at work; which of these tasks is easiest and why

- how the learner copes when he or she needs to read or write something and can't

Activity 3 Reading and Writing Needs

Ask the learner

- how the learner thinks life would be different if he or she could read and write better

- why the learner decided to improve reading and writing now

- what reading and writing tasks the learner needs to be able to do to meet personal needs

- what reading and writing skills the learner needs to improve in order to do those tasks

Abilities Needed

Assess the learner's current abilities by using some of the techniques listed below. You do not have to follow this order. Stop if the learner seems frustrated or is clearly a beginner.

Listening comprehension

Read to the learner an interesting passage that is appropriate for his or her knowledge and experience. Discuss the piece with the learner and ask questions to check understanding.

Speaking

Have a conversation to get a sense of the learner's ability to express thoughts and feelings orally.

Reading

Understanding

Show the learner several reading selections written at different levels. Then ask the learner to select one and try reading it. Afterward, ask the learner to describe what the selection was about. Ask how he or she felt about the level of difficulty and why. Ask if he or she wants to try any other selection. If the learner seems to have difficulty talking about the reading, ask him or her to read it aloud. Note the kinds of problems the learner has.

Names of numerals and letters

Point to these on a chart and ask the names (see pp. 100–101).

Oral reading

Use a piece the learner has had success with. As the learner reads it aloud, make notes about fluency, ability to keep the place, use of punctuation cues, and expression. Also note if the learner consistently makes errors that might interfere with understanding, such as guessing words based only on the initial consonant sound or mixing up sounds for certain letters.

Ability to use phonics

Check phonics in one of these three ways:

1. Ask the learner to dictate a story or experience to you. Point to individual letters, digraphs, or consonant blends. Ask the learner first to read the word and then to give the sound of the letter(s).

2. Write the alphabet, digraphs, and some sample consonant blends. Ask the learner for the sound of each.

3. Write some made-up words, such as *shup* or *cooch,* and ask the learner to sound them out.

Writing

Free writing

Ask the learner to write two to four sentences about some topic of interest. If necessary, suggest a topic related to his or her life. Ask the learner to guess at the spelling of any words he or she doesn't know for sure. Then ask the learner to read the piece aloud to you. Evaluate the legibility, spelling, punctuation, grammar, organization, and content.

Printing numerals and lower and upper case letters

Say each letter and number and ask the learner to print them on lined paper.

Using cursive writing

Ask the learner to write his or her name with cursive writing.

Writing name, address, and phone number

Activity 5 Feelings about the Assessment Process

Ask how the learner feels about the assessment process. Find out if the learner's feelings about his or her reading and writing abilities have changed. Ask if the learner was surprised about anything.

Initial Assessment Form

Date _____

Part 1: Background Information

Learner's Name _____ Age _____

Address _____

Telephone   Home _____ Work _____

Contact Information _____

Special Needs _____

Household/Family

Work Experience

Interests/Hobbies

Previous Learning Experiences

Part 2: Current Reading and Writing

What the learner thinks good reading and writing are

What the learner reads or writes now

Strategies the learner uses when faced with difficult tasks

Part 3: Reading and Writing Needs

Reasons for wanting to improve reading and writing

Things the learner needs to read and write

Things about reading and writing the learner would like to improve

Part 4: Current Abilities

(observations by both tutor and learner)

Listening Comprehension

    Strengths

    Needs

Speaking

    Strengths

    Needs

Reading

    Strengths

    Needs

Writing

    Strengths

    Needs

Part 5: Feelings about the Assessment Process

Setting Goals

Goal setting is the cornerstone of a learner-centered environment. Many of your decisions about which methods and materials to use will depend on the learner's goals. Goal setting helps both you and the learner build a framework for planning and organizing lessons and monitoring progress. As you work together, you can revisit these goals and decide when they have been met, if they need to be modified, or if the learner has new goals.

The information you obtain during the initial assessment will help you and the learner set beginning goals. If the learner finds it difficult to identify goals, it might help to review together some goals other learners have had. (See Appendix B.)

When a learner identifies a long-term goal, such as getting a good job or earning a GED, you will need to work together to break it into several short-term objectives. These objectives will allow the learner to see progress and remain motivated. You will then need to decide what activities will help the learner meet these objectives.

Be sure the activities you choose are realistic for the learner's skill level. In addition, be sure that they are concrete enough to allow the learner to see progress. The form on p. 39 is an example of how a tutor worked with Liz to set short-term objectives and select instructional activities and materials to meet them.

Liz is a young mother with two children, ages three and five. She dropped out of school in the ninth grade and now works evenings as an aide in a local nursing home. Although she has some sight vocabulary, she is a poor reader.

Teaching Adults: A Literacy Resource Book

Long-range goal: *Be able to use a checking account to pay bills*

Short-term objective #1: *Be able to read bills, locate the amount owed, and determine whom the check should be made payable to*

Activities	Methods/materials
1. Learn to recognize by sight the words: due, payable, amount, owed, balance.	1. flash cards; sentences with these words missing— learner fills in the correct word
2. Circle the payee and amount owed.	2. learner's bills; copies of other bills

Short-term objective #2: *Be able to recognize and write number words to one hundred*

Activities	Methods/materials
1. Create reference chart with numerals and matching words to keep in purse.	1. index cards
2. Read number words in meaningful context.	2. language experience story about bills paid last month
3. Match number words to numerals.	3. reference chart; index cards with word or numeral on each

Choosing Materials

You've probably noticed that, whether you are building bookshelves or cooking, the job goes more smoothly if you have the right tools. That's true of tutoring too. A good match between the learner and the materials improves communication and learning.

Types of Materials

There are four general types of materials, and tutors and learners should work together to select those that best meet their needs. Examples of each are listed below. Books mentioned by title are published by New Readers Press. (See Appendix A.)

Published Teaching Materials

- to teach specific reading and writing skills. Examples: the *Laubach Way to Reading* series, the *Challenger Adult Reading Series, Say the Word!, In the Know, Patterns in Spelling, Writing Me, TV Tutor*® (video)

- to meet the information needs and interests of adult new readers. Examples: *The Childbearing Year, A Dream with Storms* (low-level fiction), *News for You* (weekly newspaper)

Learner-written Materials

- language experience stories or free writing done as a class assignment

- writings by new readers published in literacy program newsletters or in collections, such as the two-volume *First Impressions*

Real-World Materials

Examples: newspapers, cookbooks, menus, children's storybooks, job manuals, television listings, application forms, the Bible

Tutor-produced Materials

Examples: simplified information pieces, crossword puzzles, word games, flash cards

Most tutors find that a combination of different materials often works best. For example, a learner is using the *Challenger Adult Reading Series* for primary instruction (published teaching materials). Because one of his goals is to get a promotion, he asks his tutor to help him learn to read forms he would need to complete in the new job (real-world materials). The tutor then asks him to dictate a description of the job he is seeking and turns that into a language experience story (learner-written materials). The tutor then uses both the forms and the learner's own words to reinforce the phonics skills taught in *Challenger.*

Evaluating Materials

Early in the tutoring process, you may have to select many of the materials yourself. (Check with your local library or literacy program to find out what materials they make available.) As you get to know the learner and observe his or her successes, you will get better at selecting appropriate materials. As soon as possible in the tutoring process, involve the learner in selecting and evaluating materials.

In selecting materials, consider

- your purpose, e.g., to teach a specific reading or writing skill, to give information, or to provide a pleasurable experience

- how the materials will be used, e.g., independently or with tutor assistance

- the learner's background knowledge (Learners with extensive knowledge of a topic will be more likely to be able to read something above their current reading level.)

- the readability of the materials

    The term *readability* refers to the qualities that make a reading selection easy or hard for a specific individual. In evaluating readability, you should look at both the physical format and the content of the materials. (See Appendix C.)

No materials will meet all criteria. You will have to decide which are most important and be prepared to compensate for deficiencies. For example:

- If the learner wants to read the material but is missing some important background information or skills, you can help by discussing in advance what else the learner needs to know.

- If the material includes biased information or promotes stereotypes, you can identify these sections with the learner and discuss how the author's feelings or experience might influence the author's point of view.

- If the type is too small, you can use a photocopy machine to enlarge the page or use a bar that magnifies each line.

- If the material is designed to teach specific reading skills but does not provide enough practice, you can develop additional exercises.

Using Readability Formulas

Readability formulas are an objective tool to use in evaluating the difficulty of specific material. Readability formulas give results in terms of approximate grade levels. You should not make decisions solely on the basis of grade levels, especially when working with adults. However, this information, considered along with the other criteria listed in Appendix C, can help you make initial decisions about what materials *might* be appropriate.

The two formulas described in Activities #6 and 7 are based on

- sentence length (A sentence is defined as any string of words that begins with a capital letter and ends with a period, exclamation mark, or question mark.)

- difficulty of the vocabulary

Keep the following in mind when you use a readability formula:

- Formulas give only an approximate grade level.

- Different formulas give different results.

- The grade level may differ within the material, so choose three samples—from near the beginning, in the middle, and near the end.

- Do not automatically reject materials that seem too difficult based on a formula. A learner with high need or interest may be able to read more difficult material.

- The best judge of level will ultimately be the learner.

For more information about the following formulas, see *Using Readability,* published by New Readers Press.

Activity

6 Using the Gunning Fog Index

Purpose

To determine the reading level of adult materials (The Gunning Fog Index yields a grade level that may be slightly higher than that yielded by other formulas.)

How	**Example**

1. Count about 100 words. Stop at the nearest sentence end and use the exact word count.   105

2. Count the number of sentences.   9

3. Count the number of hard words. Hard words are defined as words of three syllables or more. (Count a hard word only once in each sample. Do not count separately *-s, -ed,* or *-ing* forms of the same word, e.g., *company* and *companies.* Do not count proper names or numerals.)   7

4. Find the average number of words per sentence:

$$\frac{\text{number of words}}{\text{number of sentences}} = \text{average sentence length}$$

$$\frac{105}{9} = 11.7$$

5. Find the percentage of hard words:

$$\frac{100 \times \text{number of hard words}}{\text{number of words in sample}} = \% \text{ hard words}$$

$$\frac{700}{105} = 6.7$$

6. Find the grade level:

% hard words + average sentence length = sum

$$6.7 + 11.7 = 18.4$$

sum × .4 = grade level

$$18.4 \times .4 = 7.36$$

(seventh-grade level)

7. Repeat this process with two other samples from the same selection.

8. Average the scores for the three samples.

(Adapted from Robert Gunning, *The Technique of Clear Writing,* McGraw-Hill Book Co., 1968.)

Using the Fry Readability Graph

Purpose

To determine the reading level of written materials (Some evaluators believe that the Fry Readability Graph is somewhat more accurate with materials written below the sixth-grade level.)

How

Example

1. Count three samples of exactly 100 words, one sample each from near the beginning, in the middle, and near the end of the selection. Do not count proper names or numerals. Count around them.

$$\begin{array}{r} 9.2 \\ 11.5 \\ +12.0 \\ \hline 32.7 \end{array}$$

2. For each sample, count the number of sentences, estimating to the nearest tenth of a sentence.

3. Add together the number of sentences in the three samples. Divide by 3 to get the average number of sentences per 100 words.

$$\begin{array}{r} 10.9 \\ 3\overline{)32.7} \end{array}$$

4. Count the number of syllables in each 100-word sample. (Do not count proper names and numerals. Count -ed as a syllable even if it is not pronounced separately, e.g., *helped.*)

$$\begin{array}{r} 109 \\ 120 \\ +115 \\ \hline 344 \end{array}$$

5. Add together the number of syllables in all three samples. Divide by 3 for the average number of syllables per 100 words.

6. Plot the average number of sentences and average number of syllables on the Fry Readability Graph below. Most points should fall within the heavy lines that mark off the grade levels. If the plot falls in a gray area, the grade-level scores are not valid.

$$\begin{array}{r} 114.7 \\ 3\overline{)344} \end{array}$$

(second-grade level)

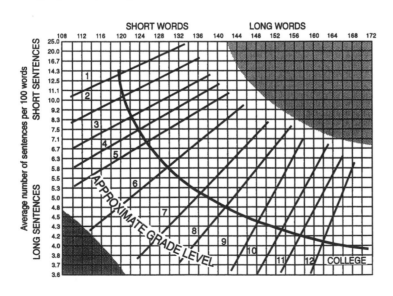

(Adapted from Edward B. Fry, "Readability Formula That Saves Time," Appendix 11-B in *Reading Instruction for Classroom and Clinic,* McGraw-Hill Book Co., 1972.)

Using Language Experience

Whenever possible, the learner needs to be involved in selecting or creating his or her own teaching materials, even if the involvement is only copying sentences or making flash cards. The Language Experience Approach (LEA) described in Activities #8–15 involves using the learner's own words to create passages to help teach reading and writing. It can be adapted for use with beginning and advanced learners. It can also be used with classes, with small groups, and in one-to-one tutoring. LEA builds on the learner's life experience and treats the learner as a person with ideas, feelings, and stories that are worth communicating. It is especially effective because it encourages the learner to use all four language acquisition-communication skills: listening, speaking, reading, and writing.

Activity 8 — Creating a Language Experience Story

Purpose

To link the learner's experience and speaking ability to the written word when the learner has little or no writing ability

How

Discuss

1. Ask the learner to share an experience.

Dictate

2. Print exactly what the learner says.

   Use correct spelling and punctuation, but do not change any words. Leave a blank line between each printed line in case you must make changes. For beginning readers, you don't need to write the whole story; three to five sentences is enough.

3. Ask the learner to suggest a title for the story.

Verify

4. Read the story back to the learner and ask for any corrections or changes.

Read

5. Read each sentence aloud, tracking the words with your finger.

6. Ask the learner to read each sentence after you.

7. Ask the learner to read the entire story.

File the story

8. Review the story at the next session. Type it, if possible, and make one copy for you and one for the learner. Place your copy in a binder or folder as part of a permanent collection of the learner's writing.

Activity 9 — Generating Story Ideas

Purpose

To generate conversations that can be used as the basis of a language experience activity

How

1. Select one of the following questions or ideas:

   • What is your favorite hobby? Describe it.

   • If you could have three wishes, what would they be?

   • What type of work do you do? What do you like and dislike about your work?

   • What is the strangest thing that ever happened to you?

   • Tell me a story about someone in your family.

- If you had as much time and money as you needed, how would you spend your vacation?

- What is something you do well? How would you tell someone else how to do it?

- What was the best choice you made in the last five years?

- What do you most like to do on your day off?

- Do you have a favorite song? Can you tell me the words?

- Tell me about your favorite television show.

- What would you say to the president if you met him or her?

- Think about someone you know. Describe what he or she looks like.

2. Use the question to start a conversation with the learner.

3. When the learner is comfortable, ask the learner to repeat an interesting piece of information so you can write it down.

Suggestion

You can also work with the learner to create a map of ideas about a particular topic. (See Activity #63.) The learner can then choose one idea to use as the basis of an LEA story or can use one map for several different stories. Maps can also help generate new ideas and topics.

Activity 10 Pictures and Photos as Story Starters

- Bring a picture to the lesson and ask the learner to describe it or ask how the learner feels about it.

- Ask the learner to bring a personal photo to the lesson and tell you what is happening in the photo.

Activity 11 Newspapers and Magazines as Story Starters

- Read an article from a newspaper or magazine to the learner. Then ask the learner to tell you about it in his or her own words.

- Read a letter from a personal advice column and ask the learner how he or she would answer it.

12 Using LEA with Beginning Readers

Purpose

To involve beginning readers in LEA activities without overwhelming them with the length or difficulty of the piece

How

1. Follow the steps for obtaining an LEA story in Activity #8.

2. Keep the selection short—only one or two sentences.

3. Read the selection aloud together (see Activity #17) before the learner tries to read it alone.

Suggestions

- Write one of the following sentence starters and ask the learner to complete it. Write as the learner dictates.

  I want _____

  I can _____

  My children are _____

  I wish _____

  I like to go to _____

  It makes me sad when _____

  When I think of my mother, I _____

- Ask the learner to dictate a short list, e.g., of the names of family members, of favorite foods, or of places he or she would like to visit.

13 Using LEA with Learners Who Have Some Writing Ability

- Instead of having the learner dictate the story to you, ask the learner to write the story on paper or on a computer with a simple word processing program. Then read the whole story to the learner; ask the learner to read it back to you.

- Have the learner copy the story in his or her own handwriting.

- Encourage the learner to explore different forms of writing. For example, ask the learner to dictate or write a letter to the editor, a classified ad, or directions to his or her home.

Activity 14   Using LEA with Groups

- Ask the group to select and discuss a topic. Then create a story on the board by asking each learner to contribute one sentence.

- Write a sentence starter on the board. Then ask each learner how he or she would complete it. Write each learner's sentence on the board.

Activity 15   Building Skills with LEA Stories

You can use LEA stories to teach many different skills. The learner is more likely to learn a skill that is connected to his or her own words. Work with the learner to choose what skill to work on. This encourages the learner to take responsibility for directing the learning. The learner can, for example:

- circle every *e* (or some other letter) in the story

- underline every capital letter

- count the number of sentences

- make flash cards for words he or she would like to learn (Ask the learner to practice until he or she can read the words by sight.)

- reconstruct one of the learner's sentences using flash cards on which you have written each word

- make as many words as possible by changing the initial consonant sound in one of the words in the story (see Activity #39), e.g., *went: bent, dent, lent*

- select words to have as sight words (You can help the learner with these words using the steps in Activity #30.)

- if there are direct quotes in the story, practice reading them with excitement, anger, sadness, boredom, etc.

- name words that begin with the same consonant blend as a word in the story, e.g., *start: stop, stuck* (You can write them down as the learner says them and then ask the learner to practice reading them.)

- select a word ending that the learner has already studied (such as *-s, -ing*), practice adding it to different words from the story, and then use each new word in a sentence (The learner can do a similar exercise by deleting endings from words in the story.)

- select a word with a long vowel sound and tell you what the word would be if the sound were changed to a short vowel, e.g., *made/mad* (You could also reverse the process, e.g., *not/note.*)

- write contractions from the story and tell you what words they stand for, e.g., *wasn't/was not*

- circle all the adjectives

- give a word or phrase that means the opposite of words you underlined in the story, e.g., tall/short, got married/got divorced

- locate on a map the places mentioned in the story

- develop a list of words to learn to spell

- identify cause and effect relationships ("Why did this happen?")

- reread the story for fluency

Note: Many of the ideas in the other activities in this book can also be used with LEA stories.

Developing Fluent Oral Reading

Many beginning readers are unsure of themselves and read haltingly with little or no expression. They often pause and wait for the tutor to tell them how they're doing. They need to develop confidence and learn to read fluently because fluent reading will improve their ability to understand and enjoy what they read. In addition, some learners have a specific goal that requires oral reading, such as reading stories to children or reading religious texts aloud.

The four oral reading techniques listed below are described in Activities #16–19. The one in Activity #16 provides the most support for the learner: the learner listens as you read aloud. The techniques in Activities 17–19 increase learner independence to where the learner is reading alone.

Reading to someone	Learner listens as tutor reads.
Duet reading	Tutor and learner read together.
Echo reading	Tutor reads and learner repeats.
Alternate reading	Tutor and learner read alternate sentences or paragraphs.

Activity 16 — Reading Aloud to the Learner

Purposes

- To allow the learner to hear someone read with good expression and phrasing

- To enable the learner to use materials that are too hard to read independently

- To provide a change of pace in the lesson
- To enable the tutor to share materials that are of personal interest, thus exposing the learner to new ideas and building the tutor/learner relationship

How

- Read aloud to the learner.
- The learner can either follow along in a copy of the material or sit next to you and look at your book.

Suggestions

- You may use materials at any reading level.
- It is more important for the learner to hear you read than to follow along word by word in the book. If the learner becomes frustrated over losing the place while trying to follow along, ask the learner simply to listen.

Activity 17 Duet Reading

Purpose

To give practice in fluent reading without putting the learner on the spot to read difficult material alone. Duet reading also helps the new reader learn to

- pay attention to punctuation marks
- develop good eye movement in order to keep the place
- read words in natural phrases
- increase the number of sight words
- read with expression
- read for enjoyment

How

(Use duet reading after the learner develops some basic sight vocabulary.)

1. **Choose something a little too hard for the learner.** Help the learner select something that is somewhat above his or her current independent reading level. The material should be on a topic of interest to the learner. It may be a book, magazine or newspaper article, pamphlet, or brochure.

2. **Begin reading together.** Sit next to the learner and read aloud together from the same selection. Read at a normal speed, using expression and

observing punctuation. The learner reads along, trying to keep up with you.

3. **Use your finger.** Move your finger beneath the line as you read to help the learner keep up.

4. **Keep going.** Continue to read at a normal rate even if the learner hesitates or falls behind. Stop if the learner stops reading completely.

5. **Don't ask questions.** Do not stop to explain the meaning of a word unless the learner asks. Do not ask any questions to check the learner's understanding. This material is to be used only as an oral reading exercise.

6. **Decide if the reading material is too hard or too easy.** If the learner keeps up easily, select more challenging material. If the material seems too difficult, use something that may be easier because it is written more simply or because the learner knows more about the subject.

Suggestions

- Use duet reading only for brief periods (7 to 10 minutes).

- Don't ask the learner to read aloud from the material alone. Since it is above the learner's independent reading level, that could be a frustrating experience.

- If you use duet reading at the beginning of a lesson, reread part of the same selection with the learner before the end of the lesson. Then the learner can see how much easier it gets with practice.

- You can also use this technique with the learner's own writing or with stories at the learner's level to practice fluent reading.

 Activity 18 Echo Reading

Purpose

To provide support by modeling the reading before asking the learner to read it aloud independently

How

1. Select material that is somewhat above the learner's independent reading level.

2. For a beginning reader, read each sentence aloud and then ask the learner to read it aloud. For a more advanced reader, model each paragraph instead of each sentence.

3. Encourage the learner to try reading independently as soon as he or she is comfortable doing so.

Suggestions

- After you both have read several sentences (or paragraphs), you might ask the learner to read the entire section again.

- You can also use this strategy with material at the learner's reading level if the learner needs help reading fluently.

- Make audiotapes of the reading selections so the learner can practice reading aloud at home. You can also use books with read-along tapes, available from various publishers. (For examples, see Appendix A.)

19 Alternate Reading

Purpose

To provide an opportunity for the learner to read aloud independently, but to give the learner breaks to relax and listen while someone else reads

How

1. Use materials that are at or slightly below the learner's independent reading level.

2. Read aloud one sentence (for beginning readers) or a paragraph (for more advanced readers).

3. Ask the learner to read the next sentence or paragraph aloud.

4. Repeat this process until you finish the passage.

Suggestions

- You may want to prepare the learner by first using either duet (Activity #17) or echo (Activity #18) reading on the same passage.

- Alternate reading works very well with plays or other material with a lot of dialog. If you use these types of materials, you might ask the learner to read only the part of a selected character.

- If you are working with more than one learner, divide the group into pairs and have them do alternate reading with each other.

Reading for Meaning

In order to obtain meaning from written material, effective readers should be able to do the following:

- recognize: match printed words with words for which they already know the meanings

- understand: understand the intended message—both what the author says and what can be inferred from the text

- react: compare and integrate the information in the text with their own knowledge and prior experience

- apply: use the new knowledge or skills gained from the reading in other contexts or to meet personal needs

Effective listeners also need to be able to do these same things.

Understanding and Reacting

A learner who can recognize all the words in a passage is not necessarily able to understand the passage or react to it using personal knowledge and experience. Several roadblocks can interfere with even the most experienced reader's ability to understand and react to reading material.

As you work with a learner, try to anticipate when these roadblocks might occur. With careful

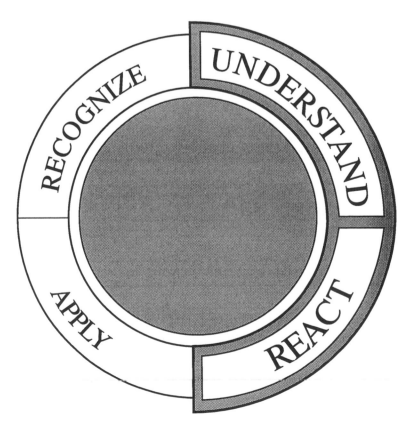

planning, you can avoid some or teach the skills necessary to get beyond them. Activities #20–29 can help you do so.

Roadblocks to understanding and reacting might include

- lack of background information (example: reading an article about a political dispute in another country without knowing any of the history leading up to it)

- unfamiliar vocabulary (example: words in directions for connecting a VCR to a television: "coaxial cable," "75/300 ohm matching transformer")

- difficulty in changing initial assumptions (example: starting to read a newspaper article titled "Running in Place" thinking it's about exercise and becoming confused when the article discusses staying in the same job for too long)

- being unfamiliar with page layout (example: not knowing how to follow the columns in a newspaper or how to find a story continued on another page)

More U.S. Troops Head for Somalia

Clinton Promises to Pull Out by March 31

President Clinton decided to double the number of U.S. troops in Somalia. At the same time, he vowed that all U.S. soldiers will be out of the African country by March 31, 1994.

Clinton's decision came after at least 15 U.S. soldiers were killed in a battle this month in Somalia's capital, Mogadishu. The body of one dead soldier was dragged by a rope through the streets of Mogadishu.

Clinton said 1,700 more soldiers will go to Mogadishu. About 3,600 Marines will be stationed on ships offshore. About 4,700 U.S. troops are already in Somalia.

"Let us finish the job we set out to do," Clinton said. "Let us show the world, as generations of Americans have done before us, that when Americans take on a challenge, they do the job right."

Many Americans believe the U.S. should pull its troops out of Somalia right away. A group of senators wants to pass a bill that would cut off funds for the mission by the end of the year.

American troops first went to Somalia in late 1992. Their mission was to bring food to millions of starving Somalis.

The U.S. mission from now until March will be to bring some order to the country. Somalia's government has collapsed. The people are ruled by a number of clan leaders.

In addition to sending more troops, Clinton also sent a diplomat, Robert Oakley. Oakley met with members of Gen. Mohammed Farah Aidid's clan. Aidid's forces have been blamed for the killings of many U.S. soldiers.

American officials say they may sit down to work out an agreement with Aidid. At the same time, they say they would capture him if they got the chance.

- overlooking details or missing a key sentence (example: failing to read the *not* in this sentence: "She did not know the name of the man who called.")

- getting lost in detail and missing the main idea (example: getting caught up in the description of something that happened to a character and missing the fact that the person is describing a dream)

- being unfamiliar with such graphic elements as diagrams, charts, or maps (example: not knowing how to read a diagram that shows how to hook up a VCR)

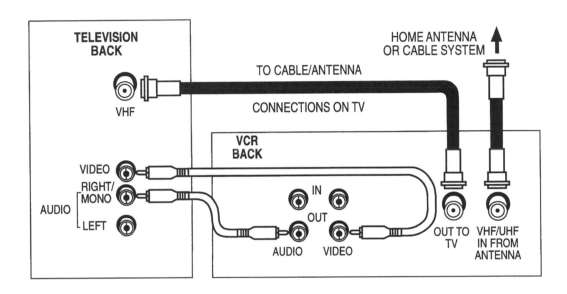

- being unfamiliar with a typeface or handwriting (example: being unable to decipher someone's handwriting or read a fancy typeface)

I'm running late. Meet me at the restaurant at 1:30

Thomas and Emily Jackson request the honor of your presence at the marriage of their daughter

- being unfamiliar with the style of writing or genre (example: reading poetry or Elizabethan English for the first time)

Activity 20 Making Predictions

Purpose

To engage the learner in the reading task and enable the learner to become an active participant in the learning

How

1. Ask the learner to make predictions at the following points:
   - the beginning of the reading ("Read the title. What do you think the story will be about?")
   - during the reading ("Do you think Sue will decide to have a baby?")
   - before the end ("Who do you think the murderer was?")
2. Write the learner's predictions in a chart like the one below.
3. Ask the learner to compare the predictions to what the text says.

Prediction	Confirmed	Disconfirmed or modified	No evidence

Suggestion

Ask the learner also to predict some of the words that might be used in the story (after reading the title, looking at any accompanying illustrations, and discussing the general content). After the learner reads the story, ask, "Did the author use those words? Why or why not?"

Activity 21 Before-During-After (Directed Reading)

Purpose

To introduce the learner to a process that readers can use to increase their understanding of written materials (See Activity #22 for suggestions about how to help a learner begin to use this process independently.)

How

Before the learner reads the selection, do the following:

1. Introduce the reading selection. Ask the learner to look at the headline, title, or headings and predict what the piece will be about.

2. Discuss the topic. Find out what the learner already knows about it.

3. Help the learner identify a purpose for reading or something to find out. Examples:

> Tutor: "Please find out what happened when Bob was late for work."
> Learner: "I'd like to know *why* the mayor is against the Police Review Board."

During the reading, do the following:

4. Encourage the learner to make predictions about content and what will happen next.

5. Help the learner correct the predictions by comparing them to what the selection actually said to check understanding.

After you and the learner have finished reading a passage do the following:

6. Discuss what the selection actually said (literal understanding).

7. Discuss what the reader had to figure out—the message between the lines (inferred understanding).

8. Identify what else the learner would like to know.

Suggestions

- Some learners may not be aware of what happens in a person's mind during reading. You can model this process by "thinking aloud" and sharing your thoughts as you read aloud to the learner.

- With longer text, ask the learner to read a section at a time using the above steps. Place a mark at the end of each section to show the learner where to stop.

Activity 22 — Creating Independent Readers

Purpose

To encourage the learner to begin to use the before-during-after strategy (Activity #21) outside of class to improve understanding while reading independently

How

Print questions on large index cards for the learner to take home as shown below.

Before I Read

1. What is this going to be about?
2. What do I already know about this topic?
3. What's my purpose for reading this?

While I Read

4. What do I think the next part is going to be about?
5. Was I right or wrong?
6. What else do I want to know about this topic?

After I Read

7. What did the article tell me?

8. What did I have to figure out?

9. What else do I want to know about this topic?

Suggestion

The learner can practice this strategy even on materials he or she cannot read alone. By reading aloud to the learner, you can also introduce the learner to a variety of types and styles of writing.

Activity 23 Asking Questions

Purpose

To help a learner go beyond literal understanding, infer meaning from the text, and add to the meaning by applying personal experience or ideas

How

After each reading, ask at least one of each of the following types of questions:

Literal questions ("What does the text say?")

Examples:

- Where did Sam go when he left the house?
- How was Sandra's family different from Jackie's family?
- List the steps involved in making a quilt.

Inferential questions ("What is written between the lines?")

These questions are not specifically answered in the text, but the reader can figure out the answer by using the literal information provided.

Examples:

- What is the main idea of the reading?
- Do you think Anne was a good mother? Why or why not?
- Can you tell whether or not Bob liked his job? How?

Applied questions ("What is in the reader's mind?")

Learners must draw upon their own background knowledge, beliefs, and experiences to answer these questions.

Examples:

- Was this an effective story or article? Why or why not?
- Do you think Maria made a good decision when she decided to marry Al? Why or why not?
- What would you have done if you were Jane?

Suggestions

- Try to ask questions that are related to each other. Your questions should lead the learner from literal understanding to a discussion of underlying ideas and how these ideas apply to his or her own experience. For example, you could ask this series of questions: "According to the article, what are the steps involved in making a quilt? What would make a person a good quilter? Do you think you could be a good quilter? Why or why not?"

- Write two or three examples of each type of question for a reading the learner will do in class. Put each question on a separate index card or piece of paper. Place them upside down in three piles. Ask the learner to select and answer questions from each pile.

- The learner can answer the questions orally or in writing depending on his or her skill level.

- If you are working with a group, ask each person to make up a question for the others to answer.

Activity 24 Tell Me What You've Read

Purpose

To allow the learner to demonstrate understanding by describing a reading passage to a partner

How

1. Choose two reading passages written at the learner's independent reading level.

2. Read one passage to yourself while the learner reads the other one silently.

3. After this silent reading, you both should describe the contents of your articles to each other.

4. Exchange passages and read the second passage silently.

5. Share your ideas about what you both read.

Note: Partners can also discuss how hearing someone talk about the passage before they read it helped them get more from their own reading of the passage.

(Adapted from Ed Robson, Marsha DeVergilio, and Donna DeButts, *LITSTART: Literacy Strategies for Adult Reading Tutors,* Michigan Literacy, Inc., 1990.)

Activity 25 K-W-L

Purpose

Used with nonfiction materials to help the learner identify what he or she already *knows* about a topic, *wants* to find out from the reading, and *learned* from the reading

How

Before the reading:

1. Prepare a form similar to the sample on p. 64.

2. Ask what the learner already knows about the topic of the article. With beginning readers, jot down ideas in the first section as you and the learner talk.

3. Review the titles, subtitles, photos, and other graphics with the learner.

4. Ask what the learner wants to find out by reading this article. You or the learner records these questions in the second section.

During the reading:

5. The learner refers to the K-W-L chart while reading. As questions are answered, you or the learner writes the answers in the third section.

After the reading:

6. You or the learner adds to the third section whatever information the learner still wants to know about the topic. Discuss where the learner can find that information.

Example

Topic/Idea/Title: A Healthy Heart

What I Know

    Too much fat is bad for the heart.

What I Want To Find Out

    How to cut down on fat in my diet.

    What foods are bad for the heart?

What I Learned (or still want to learn)

    Red meat, cheese are high in fat.

    How exercise can help my heart.

(Adapted from D. M. Ogle, "K-W-L: A Teaching Model That Develops Active Reading of Expository Text," *The Reading Teacher,* 39 (1986), 564–570.)

Activity 26 Story Map

Purpose

To make a visual outline of a story or article to help the learner understand what he or she has read

How

1. Start with a circle in the middle of the page. Have the learner write the main idea or event in that circle. (Provide assistance if the learner has difficulty writing.)

2. Help the learner map the ideas or events that spring from the center. Cluster related ideas together.

3. Encourage the learner to look back at the reading selection to see if any important ideas were missed.

Example

A learner reads a newspaper article about a proposal submitted by Triangle Construction Company to the city council. The company wants to build a new mall downtown. Bernie Malone, the council president, supported the proposal. Other members expressed concern about the mall's negative impact on the neighborhood, the increased traffic, and the effect on other downtown stores. The company vice president offered to bring a plan for how to handle the traffic to the next council meeting. The council decided to hold a public forum to discuss the mall.

The learner then works with the tutor to create the map below.

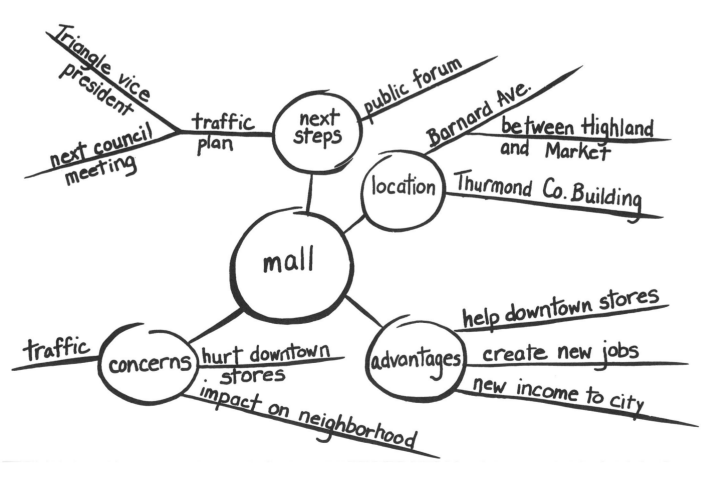

27 Reading Fiction: WWWW

Purpose

To enable the learner to understand and discuss character development, setting, and plot when reading fiction

How

1. Introduce the four *W*s and explain that the learner should be able to answer these questions about each story he or she reads.

   Who are the characters?
   Where does the story take place?
   When does the story take place?
   What happened in the story?

2. Use some of the questions or activities below to help the learner with each of the *W*s.

Who

- What kind of person was _____?

- How do you think the author felt about _____?

- How did you feel about _____?

- How did _____ change between the beginning and the end of the story? What caused the change?

- Do you know a person like _____? How is she or he like _____? Different?

- If you could meet _____, what do you think you would talk about?

- How are _____ and _____ alike in the story? Different?

- Pretend you are _____. Write (or dictate) a letter to _____ in the story to say how you feel about him or her.

Where

- Where are the characters when the story begins?

- Close your eyes and picture the setting. Describe what you see.

- Does the story happen in one place or more than one? List all the places.

- Locate the place(s) on a map.

- Have you ever been to a place like _____? What was it like?

When

- When did the story start (year, season, date, time, etc.)? How do you know?

- How much time went by between the beginning of the story and the end?

- Make a time line for the story. Write the key events on the line in the order in which they happened. Put the earliest event on the left.

- If the story took place at an earlier time in history, what do you think life was like then? What else was happening during that period?

What

- Did you know how the story would end or was it a surprise?

- What clues did the author give you that helped you guess how it would end?

- Read cards that each contain a key event in the story. Put them in the order in which they happened.

- Summarize the story in your own words.

- Pretend you are _____ in the story. Tell the story as if it happened to you.

- Draw a story map to show what happened in the story (see Activity #26).

Activity 28 Word Capsules

Purpose

To teach unfamiliar vocabulary by grouping words around a single topic or theme

How

1. List 8 to 12 important terms related to a single topic that the learner needs or wants to learn about. The list may include words from a text to be read or special sight words that the learner needs to know.

   Examples:

Banking words		Car tune-up words	
deposit	teller	carburetor	spark plugs
withdrawal	account	points	oil filter
interest	balance	timing	air filter
statement	loan	gap	idle

2. Display the list on the board or on paper.

3. Define each word and use it in context. If the words are also used in a text you are reading, point them out to the learner.

4. Ask the learner to use each word in a sentence.

Suggestions

• If you are working with a group of learners, have them pair up and take turns using the words in sentences. Then ask them to write their sentences and read the sentences aloud.

• If you are working with a beginning reader, you may want to create shorter word capsules. Ask the learner to dictate sentences using each word. Write the sentences on paper and ask the learner to recopy them.

• Encourage learners to develop their own word capsules for topics they are interested in.

• Instead of asking more advanced readers to write separate, unrelated sentences, ask them to write an entire paragraph or essay using the capsule words.

(Adapted from Mary Dunn Siedow, "Instructional Strategies" in *Teaching Adult Beginning Readers: To Reach Them My Hand,* Alan M. Frager (ed.), College Reading Association, Monograph Series, 1991.)

Activity 29 Word Charts

Purpose

To teach unfamiliar words by having the learner consider their relationships to other words

How

1. Give the learner 4" x 6" index cards or half-sheets of 8½" x 11" paper. The cards or paper should be divided into quadrants. Use one card for each new word.

New word	Definition or synonym
Association reader has with the word	Antonyms

2. Before reading, the learner writes one new word from the passage in the upper left quadrant of each card.

3. In the upper right quadrant, the learner writes the definition or a synonym for the new word.

4. In the lower right quadrant, the learner writes antonyms or opposites of the new word.

5. In the lower left quadrant, the learner writes associations with the word.

Example:

recycle	use again
This newspaper was printed on recycled paper.	throw away discard

Suggestions

- Ask the learner to keep the cards handy while reading the passage that contains the new words. The learner can refer to the cards as necessary and make additional notes in the appropriate quadrant.

- Be aware that some of the word associations may be meaningful to the learner but not to you.

Recognizing Words

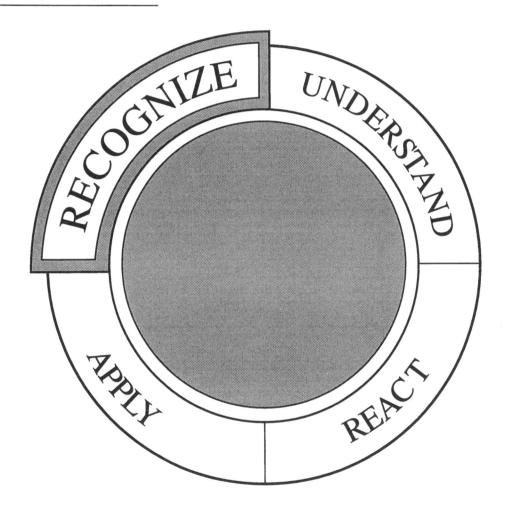

To obtain meaning from text, a person must be able to understand the author's message and react to it using prior information and experience. This can't happen, however, if the reader is unable to recognize many of the words in the text.

Recognition is the ability to match words that people see in print with words they already use and know the meaning of. Good readers are able to draw on one of five word recognition strategies to do this (see p. 71).

Sight words

Words that readers recognize instantly without having to stop to figure them out. The more proficient readers are, the more words they recognize by sight.

Phonics

The use of sound-symbol relationships to decode words.

Word patterns

The use of familiar letter groupings to help recognize parts of words.

Context

The use of the surrounding words to help figure out an unfamiliar word.

Word parts

The use of root words, suffixes, prefixes, and other word parts to recognize a word.

No one strategy works for all situations, and readers sometimes use multiple strategies to figure out a word. So the more strategies a person learns, the more likely that person is to recognize words successfully. Activities #30–49 help teach these strategies.

The strategies can be taught in any order. Start by building on what the learner already knows.

Activity 30 Sight Words

Purpose

To help the learner recognize as many words as possible by sight in order to improve reading speed and comprehension

How

1. Work with the learner to choose the words he or she wants to learn.

    Examples:

    - words the learner will use often in daily life or words from the learner's language experience stories

    - words that appear often in general writing, such as *the, there, this,* and *was*

    - words with irregular spellings that are difficult to sound out phonetically, such as *height*

    - survival words, such as family names or words that appear on forms and applications, on job-related materials, on road signs, or in public places

2. Ask the learner to print the selected words on index cards. (You can help if needed.)

3. If the learner has trouble remembering the word, ask the learner to use it in a sentence. Write the sentence. Ask the learner to copy the sentence on the back of the flash card. You can also ask the learner to draw a picture of the word on the back.

4. Ask the learner to look at each card and read it.

5. Encourage the learner to review the flash cards at home.

6. Review the words often.

Suggestions

- Teach no more than 6 to 10 new words at a time. Use fewer cards if the learner has problems with that many.

- Periodically, ask the learner to read the cards and divide them into two piles: those the learner knows and those he or she still has difficulty with. Work with the learner to reduce the size of the second pile.

- Play a game of "Beat the Clock." Time how fast the learner can read the cards. Then challenge the learner to read them again and beat the previous time.

- Set a specific amount of time. Ask the learner to read as many cards as possible in that time. Repeat the exercise to show improvement.

- See Appendix D for a list of the 300 most frequently used words. See Appendix E for a list of social sight words.

Activity **31** Phonics: Teaching Consonant Sounds

Purpose

To enable a learner to decode unfamiliar words by using knowledge of the sound-letter relationships

How

1. Select two or three words that begin with the same consonant and sound from the reading selection or the learner's language experience stories.

2. Ask the learner to write each word on a piece of paper and underline the initial consonant.

3. Ask the learner to name the letter. Teach it if necessary.

4. Say the sound of the letter, and ask the learner to repeat after you.

5. Ask for examples of other words that start with that sound, or give examples yourself.

6. Write these words on paper. Say the sound as you underline the letter at the beginning of the word. (Be careful not to use words that start with the same letter but have different sounds. Examples: *park, phone.*)

7. Have the learner practice identifying the sound in other words that are important in the learner's life.

8. If the learner has difficulty remembering a sound, ask the learner to choose a key word that will help. (Examples: *car* for *c, hand* for *h.*)

Suggestions

- Use the same technique to teach consonant blends (*st, scr*) and digraphs (*sh*).

- After the learner can identify consonant sounds at the beginning of words, repeat the process to teach consonant sounds at the end and in the middle of words.

- Review sounds taught in previous lessons.

- For additional information on teaching phonics, see *Focus on Phonics, Patterns in Spelling,* the *Laubach Way to Reading* series, and *Challenger,* all published by New Readers Press (descriptions in Appendix A).

- For assistance in teaching individual sounds, see Appendix F.

- To help you explain common phonics principles, see Appendix G. The rules are for your reference; you do not need to teach them unless you think that some might be helpful to the learner.

Phonics: Same or Different?

Purpose

To enable the learner to hear individual sounds in spoken words in order to improve decoding and spelling

How

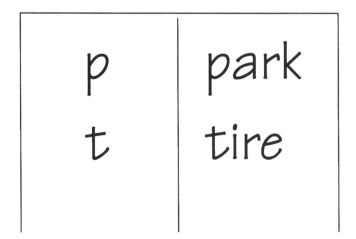

1. Select the initial consonant sounds you want to work on. List the letters in column 1.

2. In column 2, write a key word that begins with each letter. Select words from the reading selection or from the learner's language experience story.

3. Review with the learner the name and sound of each letter and the key word.

4. For each consonant do the following:

   a. Say two other words that begin with this same consonant sound. Ask the learner if the first sound is the same or different for the two words.

   b. Ask the learner what letter each of the words begins with. Ask the learner to point to that letter in column 1.

   c. Say two other words: one that begins with this same sound and one that does not. Ask the learner which one begins with the letter you are working on.

   d. Repeat the process with other pairs of words (with same or different initial sounds) until you are sure the learner can hear the sound of the letter and distinguish it from other beginning sounds.

Suggestions

- Follow the same procedure with ending consonant sounds. Then work on digraphs and beginning and ending consonant blends.

- Adapt the procedure for use with vowel sounds.

Activity 33 Phonics: Bingo

Purpose

To provide a fun way to practice reading words that begin with consonant blends

How

1. Select the consonant blends you want to work on.

2. Divide two pieces of paper into squares like a bingo card (five columns across and five columns down). See the drawing on p. 76 for an example.

3. On the first card, write a consonant blend in each of the spaces. (You can use some more than once.) Give this card to the learner.

4. Write the same blends on the second card, but put them in different places. Keep this card for yourself.

5. Select a word that starts with each blend you wrote. Write these 24 words on separate pieces of paper and put them face down in a pile.

6. Ask the learner to pick a word from the pile, read it aloud, and then give the sound of the blend.

7. Each of you should then cover the matching blend on your own card with a square of blank paper.

8. The person who first covers five blends in a row (horizontally, vertically, or diagonally) wins and becomes the "caller" for the next game.

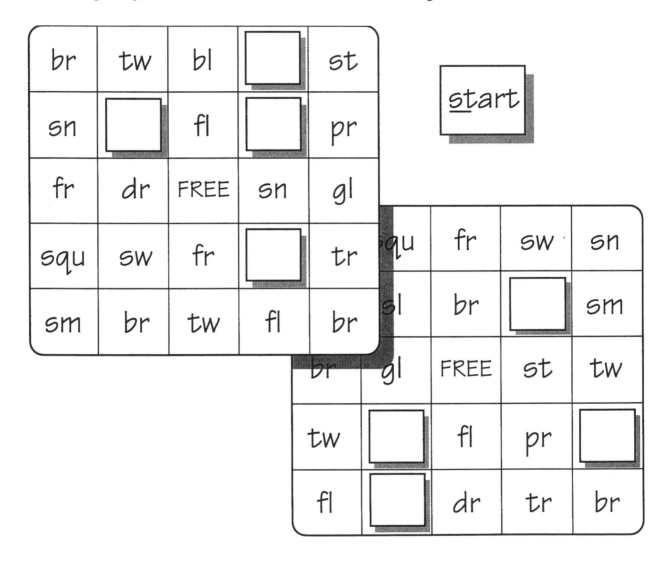

Suggestions

- This activity works well with a group.

- You can adapt the game by using words with ending consonant blends, digraphs, short vowels, *r*-controlled vowels, or any other phonic element the learner needs to practice.

Purpose

To help the learner practice vowel sounds by changing the vowel in a word to create a new word

How

1. Fold an index card in half and tape the edges opposite the fold together.

2. If you are teaching short vowel sounds, print on the outside the beginning and end of a word that could be completed with any of several short vowel sounds.

3. Cut a hole for the missing vowel.

4. Print the five vowels on a card that can be inserted into the folded index card.

5. Slowly pull the vowel card through. As each new vowel appears in the window, ask the learner to read the new word.

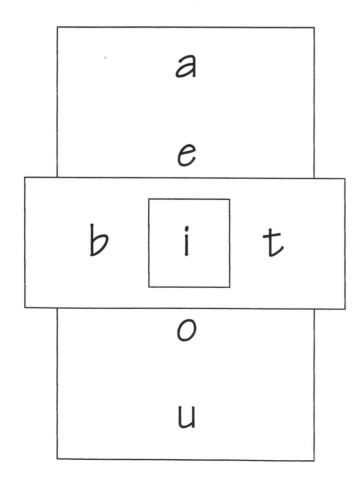

Suggestions

- You can also design the word slide so that the learner can replace the initial or ending consonant sounds.

- If the learner is uncomfortable reading nonsense words, skip over the vowels that do not make real words.

- The word slide can also be used to teach word patterns (see Activity #39).

Activity 35 — Phonics: Start with the Vowel Sound

Purpose

To encourage more careful reading by a learner who tends to look only at the first letter in a word and then guess the rest of the word

How

1. Cover all the letters in a word except the vowel. Give the vowel sound and ask the learner to repeat it.

2. Uncover the letters in the following order and ask the learner to add each new sound as you uncover it:

a	ou	a
ab	ous	ad
grab	hous	rad
	house	rade
		parade

Activity 36 — Phonics: The Disappearing Person

Purpose

To provide a fun way to help the learner practice using individual sounds to figure out a word

Teaching Adults: A Literacy Resource Book

How

1. Pick a word the learner knows.

2. Draw short lines on a piece of paper for each letter in the word.

3. Draw a stick figure in pencil next to the lines.

4. Ask the learner to guess a letter.

5. If the letter is used in the word, write it on the correct line. If not, write the letter at the top of the paper and erase one of the body parts of the stick figure (a hand, foot, leg, arm, or head).

6. The learner wins by guessing the word before you erase the last part of the figure (the body).

7. Switch roles and try to guess a word the learner picks.

Suggestions

- If you are working with a group, divide people into two teams.

- Select words that contain sounds the learner needs to practice.

Activity 37 Phonics: Decoding with Consonants

Purpose

To reduce frustration created when the learner is unsure of the correct vowel sound

How

1. If the learner comes to a word he or she can't read, ask the learner to underline each consonant and make the sound for each one.

2. Then ask the learner to blend the sounds together and try to figure out the word.

   Example:

   turtle   cabinet

3. Ask the learner to read the sentence using that word and to check if it makes sense in context.

(Adapted from Mallory Clarke, *Goodwill Literacy Tutor Handbook,* Goodwill Literacy, 1991.)

Phonics: Teaching Syllables

Purpose

To enable learners to decode complex words by breaking the words into syllables

How

1. Explain to the learner that a syllable is a word or part of a word that has only one vowel sound (not necessarily one vowel).

2. Give examples: bat (1), head (1), pa/per (2), lit/tle (2), em/ploy/ment (3).

3. Read words and ask how many vowel sounds the learner hears.

4. You can teach the three rules listed below to a more advanced learner. (This is someone who is comfortable with the meaning of syllables and would benefit from more information about them.) Stop if the activity seems too difficult or frustrating for the learner.

5. Then give the learner a list of words.

6. Ask the learner to put a dot under each vowel.

7. Ask the learner to cross out any final *e*'s.

8. Ask the learner to underline digraphs and consonant blends.

9. Ask the learner to divide the words according to the three rules.

Three rules for syllables

The two-consonant rule:

If there are two consonants between the vowels, divide the word between the consonants.

in/to   les/son   traf/fic   fen/der

Do not divide blends or digraphs.

bash/ful   em/blem

The one-consonant rule:

> If the word has only one consonant sound between two vowels, divide the word before the consonant. If the vowel comes at the end of a syllable, it will usually have the long sound.

ba/con   fe/male

The letter *y* in the middle or at the end of a word acts as a vowel.

la/dy   sy/phon

The one-consonant "oops" rule:

> Sometimes the one-consonant rule does not work. When that happens, divide the word after the consonant. The vowel will have a short sound.

lem/on   vis/it   sec/ond   ov/en   trav/el

Suggestion

- To help the learner hear the number of syllables, tap your finger on the table as you say each syllable. Later, the learner can do that independently.

(Adapted from Ed Robson, Marsha DeVergilio, and Donna DeButts, *LITSTART: Literacy Strategies for Adult Reading Tutors,* Michigan Literacy, Inc., 1990.)

Activity 39 Word Patterns

Purpose

To help the learner recognize new words more quickly without having to sound out and blend each individual sound in the word

How

1. Make sure the learner understands the concept of rhyming. Say several pairs of words and ask if they rhyme.

2. Then choose a word pattern with which you can create several rhyming words. Example: *-it*.

3. Write the word pattern at the top of a piece of paper and ask the learner to say the sound. If the learner doesn't know, say it yourself. Example: *-it*.

4. Write a rhyming word under the word pattern. Example: *sit*. Ask the learner what the word is. If the learner doesn't know, read it yourself.

5. Write another rhyming word by changing the initial consonant. Example: *bit*. Ask the learner to read it. If the learner has difficulty, give a hint: "If *s-i-t* is *sit,* then what is *b-i-t?*"

6. Keep adding words and asking the learner to read them.

7. Ask the learner to add other words using the same pattern.

8. Ask the learner to read through the entire list.

   Example:

   -it

   sit

   bit

   fit

   hit

   lit

   flit

Suggestions

- This recognition strategy can also be helpful for figuring out multisyllabic words.

  -ap *-ive*

  cap *tive*

  captive

- You can create a nonsense word and ask the learner whether or not it is a real word. But avoid nonsense words that sound like real words. Example: *cand* (canned).

- Do not confuse a beginning learner by using ending sounds that can be spelled more than one way. Examples: *fix* and *picks, tax* and *stacks.*

- When the learner is comfortable with a pattern, dictate other words that have the same pattern and ask the learner to write them.

- See Appendix H for examples of common word patterns.

Activity 40 — Word Patterns for Kinesthetic/Tactile Learners

Purpose

To involve the learner in physical activities that teach the concept of word patterns

How

Using flash cards

1. Select the word endings you want to work on. Ask the learner to write each ending on a separate index card. Examples: *-ash, -act, -ack, -ent, -each.*

2. Make a list of each of the consonants, digraphs, and consonant blends you want to work with. Ask the learner to copy each of these on a separate index card.

3. Ask the learner to place one of the consonant cards in front of a word pattern card and read the new word. (Nonsense words are allowed. The emphasis is on recognition, but you may want to discuss whether or not the new word is a real word.)

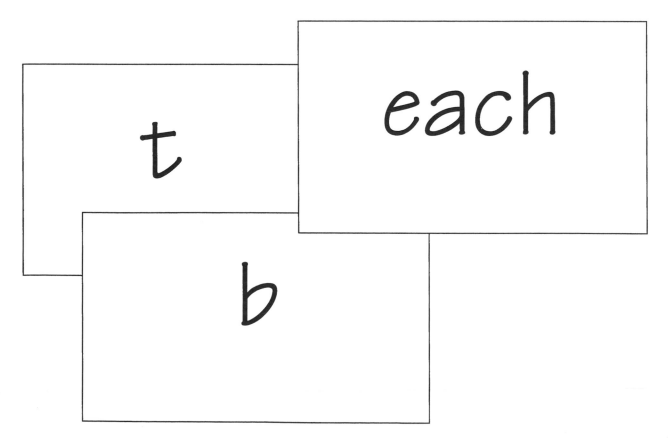

Concentration game

1. Select six pairs of words. Each pair should have the same ending pattern (one the learner has already studied). Examples: *snack/pack, dust/rust.*

2. Write each word on a separate index card.

3. Mix the cards up and lay them facedown in three rows.

4. Ask the learner to turn over two cards at a time, trying to find the two words that have the same ending pattern. Ask the learner to read each word aloud and, if the patterns match, remove the cards from the game. If not, the learner should turn them facedown again.

5. Alternate turns (the tutor and the learner or two learners) until all the cards are gone.

Suggestion: You can also use this game to help the learner recognize words with the silent *e* pattern. Examples: *bit/bite, hop/hope.*

Using a word slide

- Create a word slide like the one in Activity #34. This time, however, print a word ending on the outside. Slide a card with initial consonants through the window.

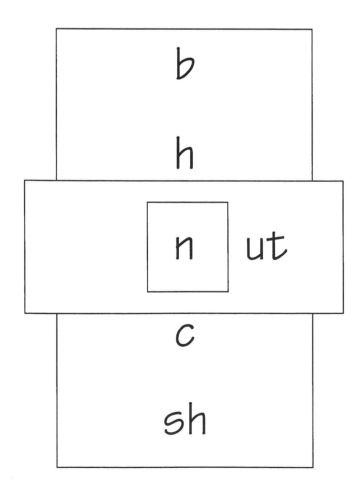

Activity 41 — Context: Just Say "Blank"

Purpose

To encourage the learner who comes to a word he or she doesn't know to continue reading and to return to the word later with more information (context) to figure it out

How

1. When the learner comes to a word he or she doesn't recognize, tell the learner to just say "blank" and keep reading.

2. Encourage the learner to use the rest of the sentence or paragraph to try to think of a word that would make sense in that place (is logical, has meaning, and is grammatically appropriate).

3. If there is more than one possibility, ask the learner to see if the first sound in the word helps narrow down the choices.

4. Ask the learner to read the sentence with the word selected to be sure it fits the context.

Activity 42 — Context: CLOZE Procedure

Purpose

To help the learner practice using context—the meaning of surrounding words and sentences—to fill in missing words in a sentence or paragraph (The word *CLOZE* comes from *closure* and means finishing or "closing" a sentence.)

How

1. You can make a CLOZE exercise by selecting a passage that is at or below the learner's current reading level. Leave the first sentence intact and then delete words in the subsequent sentences. Select words for which there are context clues. Example: "There were four eggs in the bird's _____," not "There were _____ eggs in the bird's nest."

2. Ask the learner to fill in the missing words.

Suggestions

- Remind the learner that it is most important to choose words that make sense in context. Unless the learner is working from a word list, it is not important to fill in the exact word.

- See Activity #55 for suggested CLOZE activities to teach writing.

43 Context: Using CLOZE with a Beginning Reader

Purpose

To provide additional support to help the beginning reader be successful with the CLOZE exercise described in Activity #42

Suggestions

- Keep the passage short.

- Delete very few words and no more than one per sentence.

- If necessary, provide a word list for the learner to choose from.

- Use material with which the learner is already familiar, such as a language experience story or a passage from a previous lesson.

- If the material is new, give the learner an overview of the contents before he or she starts reading.

- Provide the first letter for each word deleted.

- Delete only one kind of word, such as nouns, in each passage. Tell the learner what kind of word you deleted.

- Provide a choice of two words for each blank. You can also write the first letter of the word in the blank space so that the learner has both context and phonics clues.

- Provide the exact number of spaces for the deleted word.

- Ask the learner to say the missing word rather than write it.

- Ask the learner to explain why that word seems to be a good fit.

Word Parts: Compound Words

Purpose

To help the learner put words together to form compound words

How

1. Select five or six compound words that are made up of smaller words that the learner can already read.

2. Put the first half of each word in one column.

3. Put the second half of each word in a second column.

4. Ask the learner to connect the two words that form a compound word and then read the new word.

5. If you're not sure that the learner recognizes the word, ask the learner to use it in a sentence.

   Example:

   pay   plane

   air   room

   bed   house

   grand   check

   tree   mother

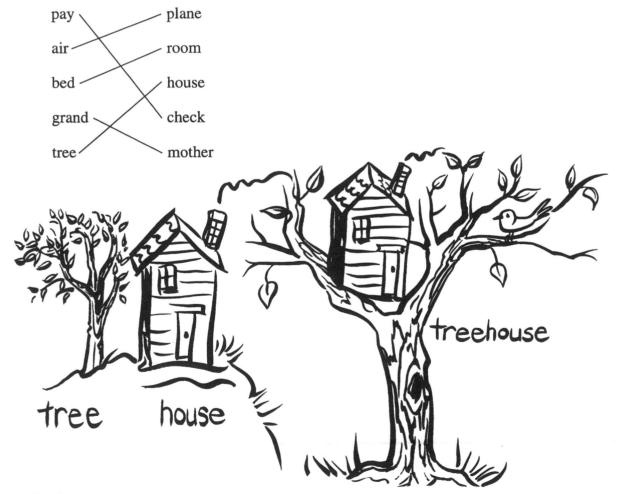

treehouse

tree   house

Activity 45 Word Parts: Distinguishing between Plural and Possessive Endings

Purpose

To help the learner distinguish between the plural and possessive noun endings

How

(Use only after the learner has had a chance to read both plural and possessive words in context and has discussed how the endings affect the meaning of the word.)

1. Make three columns on a paper.

2. In the first column, list five or six nouns that the learner already knows. Ask the learner to read them.

3. Write *s* at the top of the second column.

4. Write *'s* at the top of the third column.

5. Read a sentence using the plural or possessive form of the word in column 1.

6. Ask the learner to write the word under the correct column heading.

   Example:

   Ann is the boy's mother.

	-s	's
boy		boy's
girl		
doctor		
cat		
mother		

Suggestion

• You can adapt this activity to teach other word parts. Examples: *s/es, d/ed.*

Activity 46 Word Parts: Adding Endings to Words

Purpose

To help the learner select the correct rule when adding endings to words

How

1. Select the ending you will work on. Example: *-ing*.

2. Select the type of word to which you will add the ending. Example: verbs that end in *e*.

3. Explain to the learner the rule for adding the ending to this type of word. Example: When the word ends in *e*, drop the *e* before adding *-ing*.

4. Make two columns on a sheet of paper. In the first column, list four to six words that illustrate the rule you just taught.

   Example:

give	giving
live	living
love	
bake	
race	
shine	

5. Ask the learner to read the first word and tell you what the word would be if the ending were added. Then write that word in the second column, or ask the learner to write it.

6. Ask the learner to do the rest of the words alone.

7. Finally, ask the learner to say a sentence using the words in each column.

Suggestions

- You can modify this activity to fit almost any word ending.

- With a beginning reader, create a list where the learner applies the same rule to each word (as in the example above).

- With a more advanced learner, you can mix the words. Ask the learner to decide which rule to use before adding the ending. Example: *give, hit, kick.* Ask the learner to say the word with the ending *-ing* and then apply the correct rule to write the new word (*giving, hitting, kicking*).

- See Appendix G for rules for adding endings.

 Activity 47 Word Parts: Prefixes

Purpose

To help the learner recognize how adding a prefix changes the meaning of a word

How

1. Select the prefix you want to work on and discuss its meaning.

2. List words that begin with that prefix in the first column. Help the learner read them.

3. In the second column, write sentences using words the learner already knows. Leave a blank for the missing word.

4. Ask the learner to select the correct word from the first column to complete each sentence.

   Example:

   ....

   unhappy   I left in a hurry with the beds _____ .

   uncomfortable   I found two _____ bills on the table.

   unmade   She seemed _____ in the movie.

   unpaid   The chair was hard and _____ .

   uninterested   He looked tired and _____ .

   ....

Teaching Adults: A Literacy Resource Book

Suggestion

- See Appendix I for a list of prefixes and suffixes and their meanings.

48 Word Parts: Changing Root Words

Purpose

To help the learner understand how adding a prefix or suffix to a root word can change its meaning

How

1. Select five or six words that have both a prefix and a suffix.

2. Ask the learner to underline each prefix and circle each suffix.

   Examples:

3. Ask the learner to use the root word in a sentence. Write the sentence, or ask the learner to do it.

4. Ask the learner to use the root word with the suffix in a sentence. Write the sentence.

5. Ask the learner to use the word with both the prefix and the suffix in a sentence. Write the sentence.

6. Discuss how adding the prefix or suffix changed the meaning of the word.

7. Do the same for each word.

Activity 49 Word Parts: Contractions

Purpose

To help the learner recognize that a contraction is made up of two other words

How

1. Write several sentences that use contractions.

2. Ask the learner to read each sentence and underline the contraction. (Read the sentences to the learner if he or she has trouble.)

3. Ask the learner to write the two words that make up the contraction next to each sentence.

> Examples: Her mother <u>isn't</u> going to say yes. is not
>
> He <u>can't</u> get these until noon. can not

Applying New Skills to Meet Everyday Needs

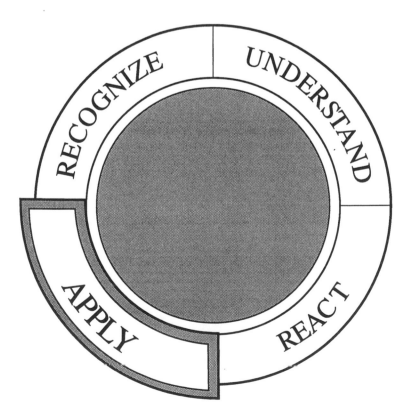

Good readers are able to apply information they learn from reading to help them meet their everyday needs. One of the tutor's major responsibilities is to design activities that help the learner build bridges between the tutoring sessions and the learner's daily life.

50 From Here to There

Purpose

To give the learner practice in reading words related to giving directions: *right, left, straight, street, blocks, turn,* etc.

How

1. With the learner, make a map of the learner's neighborhood. Include street names. (Before doing this, you might have to introduce the learner to the concept of maps and how they are used.)

2. Add where the learner lives. Ask the learner to identify several other land-marks: a grocery store, post office, factory, school, park, etc. Add these to the map.

3. Write directions from the learner's home to one of the landmarks, but do not name the destination.

4. Ask the learner to follow the map while reading the directions and then identify the destination.

Suggestions

- Reverse roles and ask the learner to write the directions. (A beginning writer can dictate them to you.)

- When working in a group, divide learners into pairs. Ask everyone to write a note to their partner with directions to their home.

51 Making a Grocery List

Purpose

To help the learner read the grocery ads in a newspaper and words related to food

How

1. Cut a page of grocery ads from your newspaper.

2. Make a shopping list of 10 to 12 items listed in the ads.

3. Ask the learner to find the items in the ads and write the price on the list next to each item.

4. Ask the learner to add the prices and find out what the total bill will be. Provide help if needed.

Suggestions

- Reverse roles and ask the learner to make a grocery list for you from the words in the ad.

- Cut the food words out of the paper. Ask the learner to categorize them and show what section of the store they can be found in (e.g., meat, dairy, or produce).

Activity 52   Building Bridges

Purpose

To help the learner see how information from the tutoring session can be applied to a variety of real-life activities

Suggestions

- Bring in a movie schedule and practice finding the time and place of a particular movie.

- Bring in a TV schedule and find the time and channel of various programs.

- Read washing instructions on an item of clothing.

- Go to the store and choose a greeting card for a friend's birthday.

- Read a bus schedule and figure out what bus you would need to take to reach your destination by 3:00 p.m.

- Read directions on a food package.

- Clip and use grocery coupons.

- Locate newspaper job ads of interest.

- Read the recommended dosages on an over-the-counter medication.

- Chart your family tree.

- Copy signs on your street. Practice reading them in class.

- Read about an interesting person or place.

- Practice reading a storybook so you can read it to your child.

- Read a letter to a columnist. Write or dictate your own answer. Then compare it with what the columnist actually said.

- Learn a new game by reading the directions.

Writing for Meaning

Writing, like speaking, is an opportunity to send a message, to express something to someone else. In order to communicate effectively, writers or speakers have to know who their audience is, what they want to say, and how to say it so that their message is clear to the audience.

Writing can be intimidating to someone who has never written more than his or her name. It is risky business to begin expressing yourself in a new way, a way in which you have been silent all your life. Tutors can help by encouraging the learner to first concentrate on meaning. Spelling, punctuation, and grammar will come with practice. (In the meantime, see the description of invented spelling in Activity #66.) These should not be the most important skills for a beginning writer. The learner will be more willing to take chances when the tutor emphasizes the strengths instead of the mistakes.

The writing activities (Activities #53–65) provide varying degrees of support for the learner. Although they are generally listed in order of difficulty, you can easily adapt any one to meet the needs of a specific learner. They cover

- letter formation
- copying
- controlled writing
- free writing

 Activity 53 Letter Formation: Five Steps to Printing

Purpose

To teach printing to learners who have not had much practice using the fine muscles of their hands

How

1. Select a word that contains the letter the learner wants to work on. Read the word and review the name and sound of the letter if necessary.

2. First demonstrate each stroke needed to print the letter. Make the strokes in the air. Then ask the learner to do it with you.

3. Make the strokes on unlined paper. Then ask the learner to copy them.

4. Write the whole letter on unlined paper. Describe the letter as you make it. Then ask the learner to print the letter.

5. Trace the letter on lined paper. Use paper with three guidelines. Explain that all letters stand on the bottom guideline. Some letters start from the top guideline and some from the middle guideline. Some letters descend below the bottom line. Then print the letter on the guidelines and ask the learner to trace it.

6. Write the letter on lined paper. Ask the learner to use a pencil to practice printing the same letter several times on the guidelines.

Suggestions

- Teach only the letters the learner does not know.

- Whenever possible, link the writing to the reading.

- It isn't necessary to teach the letters in alphabetical order. You might help the learner learn to print the letters in his or her name first. You can also ask if there are letters the learner would like to start with.

- Make sure the learner has plenty of room on the table for paper and arms and that the chair and table are at a comfortable height. Be sure there is enough light as well.

- Provide a pencil with an eraser. Many learners do not like to have mistakes or messy papers. The pencil will be easier to use if it has a somewhat dull point, because new writers tend to exert a lot of pressure.

- Limit writing practice for beginners to prevent hand fatigue and cramps. Limit the number of new letters you introduce in each lesson.

- Keep a sample printing chart (see pp. 100–101) on the table for reference until the learner can write all of the letters and numbers independently.

- If he or she is having a lot of difficulty remembering the shape of a letter, ask the learner to describe the shape and relate it to a familiar object as a memory "key."

  Examples: *O* is round like an orange, *J* looks like a fishhook.

- If necessary, give extra practice by asking the learner to trace the letters in sand. You can also cut the letters out of sandpaper and ask the learner to trace them with a finger. These techniques are especially helpful for kinesthetic/tactile learners.

- You can adapt this process to teach cursive writing after the learner is comfortable and proficient with printing.

- Letters can look very different depending on the typeface used. To help the learner recognize letters in a different kind of type, select examples of different styles of a letter from magazines or newspapers. Cut them out and paste them on a sheet of paper. Make a separate sheet for each letter. As an alternative, ask the learner to find and cut out these examples.

Teaching Adults: A Literacy Resource Book

The Lowercase Letters

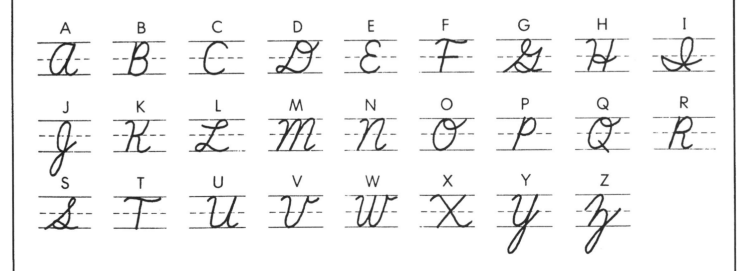

a b c d e f g h i

a b c d e f g h i

j k l m n o p q r

j k l m n o p q r

s t u v w x y z

s t u v w x y z

The Capital Letters

A B C D E F G H I

A B C D E F G H I

J K L M N O P Q R

J K L M N O P Q R

S T U V W X Y Z

S T U V W X Y Z

Numbers

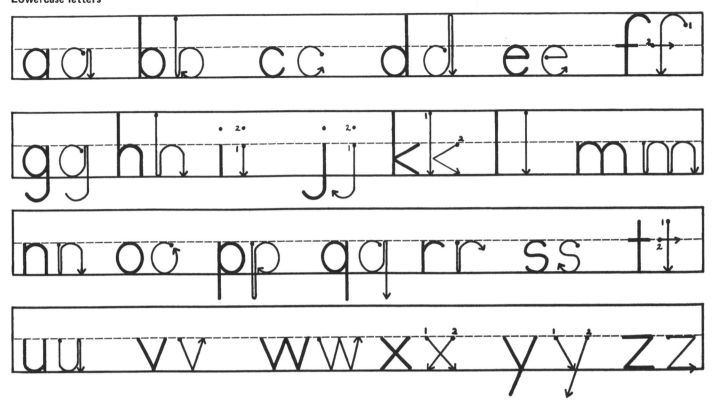

Copying

Purpose

To help the learner become comfortable with writing words and sentences
(These ideas are nonthreatening and can be done in class or for homework.)

Suggestions

- Ask the learner to read something and circle the words he or she wants to learn. Ask the learner to copy them onto separate index cards for sight word practice.

- Ask the learner to copy all the traffic signs on his or her street. Then review them together.

- Ask the learner to copy a language experience story that he or she dictated. (See Activity #8.)

- Ask the learner to dictate a note to a friend or relative, copy it, and mail it.

- Help the learner make a vocabulary list related to a reading. Ask the learner to dictate sentences using these words and then to copy the sentences.

- Make a crossword puzzle with words the learner knows. The learner can copy the words into the puzzle from a word list you provide.

- Select activities that reinforce a reading, or work with topics of interest to the learner.

- Keep copying activities short. Ask the learner to copy only materials that have personal value.

Controlled Writing: CLOZE Exercises

Purpose

To help a learner who can copy words and sentences begin to use writing to communicate meaning (Activity #42 shows how to use CLOZE exercises to develop context skills needed for effective reading.)

Suggestions

- Ask the learner to complete sentences by selecting from a word list.

  Example:

  I asked _____ to get _____ from the store (bread, Fred).

- Write a list of words and a sample sentence. Ask the learner to write the sentence several times, using a different word in the blank each time.

  Example:

  brother   sister   father   mother   mechanic

  My _____ fixed the brakes on the car.

  My mother fixed the brakes on the car.

- Ask the learner to dictate a description of an experience or something else or instructions for doing something. For example, ask the learner to give you directions from his or her home to the post office. Then rewrite those directions as a CLOZE exercise. You may choose to include a choice of words for each blank.

Teaching Adults: A Literacy Resource Book

Example:

Turn _____ (right, left) at the light at the corner of Maple and _____ (Grant, Oak). Walk three _____ (blocks, streets). The post office is just past the _____ (Laundromat, hardware store).

- Select a paragraph from a passage the learner has read. Rewrite or type it as a CLOZE exercise. If necessary, provide a list of words from which the learner can choose.

Activity 56 — Controlled Writing: Filling Out Forms

Purpose

To encourage the learner to use writing to meet practical needs

How

1. Collect samples of the type of form you want to work on (such as employment applications from area businesses).

2. Work with the learner to fill out one of the forms.

3. Ask the learner to complete another form independently using the information from the one you did together. Provide help as needed.

Suggestions

- Practice writing checks. Ask a bank for sample checks or make several copies of a form that looks like a real check. Give the learner a list of bills to be paid. Include the name of the person or company and the amount owed. Ask the learner to write a check for each bill. Provide a reference chart with the number words if needed.

- Clip coupons for free items from newspapers and magazines. Ask the learner to fill them out and mail them. Then use what the company sends as part of a future reading lesson.

- Consider other forms, such as catalog order forms, voter registration forms, library card applications, health history forms, and school permission forms.

Activity 57 Controlled Writing: Sentence Completion

Purpose

To provide structured activities to help the learner begin using writing to communicate ideas

How

1. Prepare a number of open-ended sentences.

   Examples:

   When I think of my mother, I feel _____.

   My favorite color for a car is _____.

2. Ask the learner to copy the beginnings of the sentences and then to complete them with a single word or phrase.

3. Ask the learner to read the sentence to you and to explain why he or she selected that word or phrase.

Suggestion

- Write questions for the learner to answer with complete sentences. To start, select questions that can be answered with information in the reading selection. Then move on to questions that do not require a specific answer.

  Examples:

  When will Soo-Lin arrive home?

  Soo-Lin will arrive at 5:30.

  What is your favorite season?

  My favorite season is summer.

Teaching Adults: A Literacy Resource Book

Controlled Writing: Making Lists

Purpose

To help the learner use lists to organize activities or remember important information

How

1. Ask a question or set a task related to a reading or to the learner's life.

   Examples:

   List the names of people in your family.

   List the jobs you have held and the dates you worked in them.

   List the names on your Christmas list and what you will get each person.

   Make a list of chores for family members.

   Make a list of items you need at the grocery store.

   Name the tools you need to fix a flat tire.

   Make a list of what you have to do this week. Include the day and time.

2. Discuss the list with the learner. Is the list complete? Has anything been left out that should be added?

Suggestion

- Help the learner start keeping a calendar for writing appointments, meetings, or special events to remember.

Activity 59 Free Writing: Journals

Purpose

To encourage the new writer to use writing to express thoughts and feelings without having to share them with anyone else

How

1. The learner will need a separate lined notebook to use for this journal.

2. Explain that journals or diaries serve as a record of an event or as a place to express feelings or ideas. Add that journals are private; the learner shares them only if he or she wants to.

3. Provide time in each lesson for the learner to write in the journal. Encourage the learner to make additional entries at home.

4. Tell the learner not to worry about spelling or punctuation. You can answer any questions, or the learner can guess.

5. Explain that the entry can be as short or long as the learner chooses.

6. Suggest topics if necessary.

   Examples: the weather

   what the learner did during the day

   how the learner feels about the tutoring; what the learner is getting out of it

   something special that happened during the week

Jan 4   it is col todda lots of sno.

Jan. 7   i got a nyo cot   it is red

Jan. 11   i wen to see the moov Abot 2 pepl livin in the maotins.   They mad frends with the wuls.

Jan 14   im doing good I lik reding with Jak. but I don lik writing.

Suggestions

- Model journaling by keeping a journal while the learner is writing during class.

- Ask the learner to review the journal monthly. The learner will be able to see how the entries have changed and writing skills have improved.

Free Writing: Dialog Journals

Purpose

To provide an opportunity for the learner to communicate with another person by means of reading and writing instead of listening and speaking

How

1. Use a separate lined notebook.

2. Explain to the learner that the dialog journal is a way to communicate in writing.

3. Begin by writing an entry yourself. End it with a question. Ask the learner to answer the question and then write a question for you to answer. Tell the learner not to worry about punctuation, spelling, and grammar.

4. In your response, use correct spelling or punctuation to model something the learner has a problem with. (See the sample on p. 108, in which the tutor models the correct spelling of *party* and *years*.) You don't need to call attention to the correction.

5. Regularly look through the dialog journal with the learner to discuss how his or her writing has improved. You might also mention those improvements in some of your responses in the journal.

Suggestions

- It is important that you always respond in some way to the learner's journal comments.

- You and the learner can write in the journal either during the lesson or at home.

- Share some of yourself in your responses; write about your friends, family, thoughts, and problems.

- Encourage the learner to discuss problems with reading and writing, favorite books, or things he or she does well.

- If you are working with a group, ask the learners to work in pairs to create dialog journals.

August 10   Bobby is 5 yers ol and wer haveing a parte

My son Mark is 29 years old. Will you get Bobby a present for his party?

a bik with 2 weels

December 13   I'm feeling sad today. My mother is in the hospital. How are you feeling?

I feel god yur mother wat do she hav

December 14   she has cancer and might die. I hope the doctor will have some good news for me today. Do you know anyone with cancer?

December 15   I hope so to cancer is bad. my fend Bill die from cancer He was my fend from wen we wer litle

Teaching Adults: A Literacy Resource Book

Activity 61

Free Writing: A Five-Step Process

Purpose

To develop a process that allows the learner to communicate clearly and effectively by focusing first on the content and only later on correctness

How

1. **Rehearse**

   Decide what to write about.

   Ideas may come from conversation between you and the learner, a practical need (e.g., to write a note to a child's teacher), or thoughts generated from reading. Brainstorming (in Activity #62) and mapping (in Activity #63) are good ways to stimulate or organize ideas. The topic should be something of interest to the learner or draw on the learner's experience and expertise.

2. **Draft**

   Get it down on paper without worrying about whether it is correct.

   For the first draft, the learner focuses on the message rather than on punctuation, grammar, spelling, or handwriting. A learner who has difficulty spelling a word can use invented spelling (Activity #66), draw a symbol, or simply ask for help.

3. **Revise**

   Clarify and expand the content.

   Help the writer improve the work by discussing it. There are many different approaches you can take:

   • Ask the learner what the piece is about, who the audience is, and what that audience should know, feel, or learn from the writing.

   • Ask the learner to read the piece to you and then discuss the content. This is especially helpful if the learner is embarrassed about spelling or handwriting. It isn't necessary for anyone else to see the first draft.

   Use the following questions:

   "Is the topic clear?"

   "Are there enough supporting details, examples, or reasons?"

"Can any details be added, changed, or taken out to make the ideas clearer?"

"Are all ideas arranged in a logical order?"

- Ask the learner to listen critically as you read the pieces. Then ask, "Does it say what you want it to say? What do you like best about it? How can you improve it?"

Whatever form this feedback session takes, remember to praise. Make suggestions in the form of questions:

"What would happen if . . . ?"

"How would it sound if . . . ?"

"How could you help the reader to better (see, hear, imagine) . . . ?"

"How would you summarize in one sentence what you (felt, thought, imagined) when this happened?"

"What else did you (notice, feel, say) when this happened?"

After discussing the draft, the learner may be satisfied with it. If not, the learner can revise the piece as often as necessary until the content is acceptable. The learner decides what to change.

4. Edit

Make final improvements or corrections.

The learner may revise the pieces several times. After the content is satisfactory, the learner can focus on the mechanics—spelling, punctuation, and grammar. The type and amount of editing depends on the purpose of the piece and its audience. A note to a close friend does not need to be edited as strictly as a letter to a possible employer.

You can help the learner edit the writing by focusing on only one thing at a time, perhaps the use of capital letters, periods, or commas. Your task is to help the new writer improve, not to make the writing perfect! Too much editing could undermine a new writer's confidence and feelings of success about writing. Take care not to be overwhelming. (See additional suggestions in Activity #65.)

5. Publish

Share the writing with others.

Learners begin to see themselves as writers when they use writing to meet their communication needs and when other people read and react to their ideas and experience.

For a new writer, "publishing" a piece means sharing it with another person. It can mean giving a piece to the tutor to read. It can also mean

110

sending a letter or note to someone, posting something on the literacy program's bulletin board, or publishing an item in a newsletter or collection of writings by new writers.

Suggestions

- This writing process can be used with people who are just learning to write as well as with learners who have more skill. Beginning writers can dictate the first draft as a language experience story. (See Activity #8.)

- A learner who has access to one might write, revise, and edit on a computer with a simple word processing program.

- This writing process may take several sessions. The writer can also stop the writing process at any time. A learner may no longer be interested in the topic, no longer have a need for the piece of writing, or have a new item to write that is more important.

- Keep samples of the learner's writing in a separate folder. Help the learner to see how the writing changes and improves. (See Activity #65.) Remind the learner that writing is a process, not just a product.

62 Free Writing: Brainstorming

Purpose

To help the learner generate ideas to use in writing (This activity can be used as part of the rehearsal step in Activity #61.)

How

1. Write a word or topic at the top of a page.

2. Ask the learner to write or dictate as many ideas as possible about this topic.

3. Don't discuss or evaluate any of the ideas. Every idea is valid.

4. When the learner begins to run out of ideas, see if the ideas already listed stimulate other thoughts.

5. When the learner completes the brainstorming, review the list together. Ask the learner to select ideas or topics to use in the writing.

Suggestions

- Use brainstorming to generate ideas for topics or to list points the learner wants to include about a specific topic.

- If you are working with a group, invite people to call out ideas as you write them on the board. Remind them not to comment on any of the ideas until the activity is complete.

Bad Weather

floods

too cold

too hot

thunderstorms

tornados

hurricanes

fog

Free Writing: Mapping

Purpose

To provide a visual image of a person's ideas and how they relate to each other (This activity can be used as part of the rehearsal step in Activity #61.)

How

1. Write a word or topic in the center of the page and circle it.

2. Ask the learner what comes to mind when thinking about the topic.

3. Write what the learner says. Group related ideas using circles or lines to show connections.

4. Talk about the finished map and make additions or revisions.

5. Ask the learner to identify parts of the map to include in the writing.

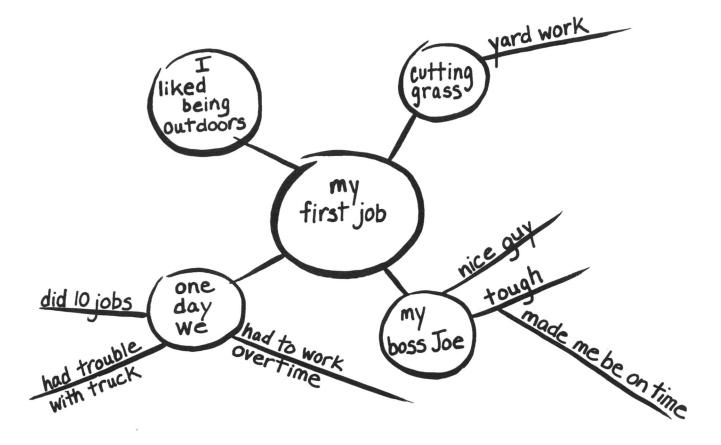

Suggestions

- For beginning writers, do all the writing and read the results back to the learner. This frees the learner up to think.

- A more advanced writer might be able to do the mapping. You can ask the learner questions to help expand or clarify the map.

- To help the learner get comfortable with maps, you might want to work together to make a map of a reading selection you've completed. See Activity #26.

- Ask the learner to brainstorm thoughts about a specific topic and dictate them to you. Go over the list, and ask the learner which ideas belong together. Mark these items or write them in clusters. Then work together to prepare a map. (This procedure gives the learner more control over how the ideas are related.)

Activity 64 — Free Writing: Say It a Different Way

Purpose

To encourage the learner to explore different forms and styles of writing

Suggestions

Have the learner

- take the role of a character in a story he or she just read and write a letter to another character in the story

- select a portion of a fiction story and create a play with dialog

- write a letter to the editor about an article in the newspaper

- write a news article about a sporting event or something that happened in the community

- write instructions for making something simple

- write a critique of a book or movie

- cut out comic strips from the newspaper, cover the words, and write new ones

Note: Learners may be uncomfortable with certain of these activities. Be sure they have enough background or experience with an activity before you decide to use it. For example, do they know how to read comics or what a written play looks like?

Activity 65 — Keeping a Writing Folder

Purpose

To provide evidence of improvement in a learner's writing; to help the learner track improvement in specific skills; to help the learner edit future writings independently

How

1. Choose a folder, three-ring binder, or box for the learner's writings.

2. Make editing notes about the skills you have worked on together. (You can use the inside front cover or separate pages in the folder.) This list

should include specific grammar, punctuation, or spelling skills. Add to the list as you identify new things to work on. Choose codes that you and the learner can both use to represent different kinds of errors. (See the example below.)

3. The learner should review the editing list and use it to correct the next piece of writing.

4. Ask the learner to use the codes to mark other words or places in the writing that might need to be corrected (if the learner isn't sure).

5. Review the learner's work. Mark other uncaught errors that relate to the editing list or to new skills you'd like to focus on. Help the learner make corrections if needed.

6. Work with the learner to decide what to keep in the folder. (See the suggestion below.)

7. Review the folder periodically and invite the learner to note improvement and what needs more work.

8. Invite the learner to add new pieces or delete old pieces so that the folder reflects progress as he or she sees it. (See "Portfolios" in the chapter "Evaluating Progress" for ideas about using a portfolio to track progress.)

Suggestion

You might include the following items in the folder. Date each piece so you can see changes or improvements.

- drafts, revisions, and final copies (stapled together)

- unfinished pieces (The learner might want to return to these later.)

- ideas for other writing activities

Editing List

Spelling
  letter
  understand

Capital letters start   Ⓣhe keys are in the car.
a sentence

Punctuation   I am 49⬚
  sentence ends with a **.** or **?**   How old are you⬚

Spelling

Many learners are intimidated by writing because they don't spell very well. But spelling and writing are two very different tasks. Writing is expressing oneself on paper. Spelling is simply a tool that helps the reader recognize individual words. A good speller is not necessarily a good writer, and some of the best writers are not very good spellers.

Inability to spell should not prevent a learner from beginning to write. Spelling is more important in some situations than in others; it depends on the intended audience. For example, spelling is not too important in a personal journal, but it is very important in a job application.

Follow these general practices in helping learners cope with spelling:

- Set aside some time each week to work on spelling.

- Ask the learner to select words he or she wants or needs to be able to spell. (The words should be from a piece of the learner's writing.) Decide how to teach the words (phonics, word patterns, word parts, etc.). Then create brief exercises that use them. This helps the learner see the relationship between reading and writing.

- Use multisensory teaching techniques. (See pp. 25–26.)

- Select words that are already in the learner's speaking and listening vocabularies.

- Select words that were used in a reading selection or the learner's language experience story.

- Select words that the learner uses frequently in writing.

- Encourage the learner to correct his or her own spelling as much as possible.

For additional assistance with spelling, see *Focus on Phonics* and *Patterns in Spelling,* published by New Readers Press (described in Appendix A).

Activity 66 — Invented Spelling

Purpose

To encourage the learner to make an educated guess about how to spell a word; to prevent the learner from getting hung up on a word and too frustrated to continue writing; to identify the words the learner wants and needs to be able to spell correctly

How

1. Ask the learner to write as much of the word as possible.

2. Ask the learner to draw a line for the letter(s) he or she doesn't know.

    Examples:

    t _ f
    f _ zi __ n
    r _ nkls
    fl _ r

3. Ask the learner to fill in the missing letters as if the word were spelled just as it sounds.

    Examples:

    t u f
    f i zishun
    rinkls
    fl o r

4. When the learner has finished writing, work together to correct the parts of the words that are still misspelled.

5. Look for patterns in the learner's mistakes. Group those words together and focus on teaching the skill the learner needs. This step is especially important for adults, who will often be judged by their ability to spell words correctly.

   Example: You might help a learner practice writing words that have a silent *w: wrinkle, write, wrong, wring.*

Activity 67 Spelling: Test/Correct/Study/Retest

Purpose

To teach the learner a whole-word approach to spelling that encourages self-correcting (This approach is especially useful for a visual learner.)

How

Test

1. Create a list of 5 to 10 spelling words that the learner wants or needs to know how to spell. The words should be part of the learner's reading, listening, and speaking vocabularies.

2. Say each word, use it in a sentence, and ask the learner to write the word.

Correct

3. Say each word and spell it out loud so the learner can check the spelling. Have the learner mark any misspelled word.

4. As you spell the word out loud, have the learner write the correct spelling next to the first attempt.

Study

5. Have the learner study only the words that were misspelled. Ask the learner to say the word out loud, spell it out loud, close his or her eyes and visualize the word, look at the word again, cover the word, write it, check it against the correct spelling, and write it again.

Retest

6. Repeat the testing process on the words that were misspelled the first time.

7. Discuss the results with the learner.

Activity 68   Creating a Spelling Dictionary

Purpose

To enable a beginning learner who has had trouble using a published dictionary to create a personal dictionary of words he or she needs to write at home or on the job

How

1. Use a small three-ring notebook (so pages can be added as needed).

2. Write one letter of the alphabet at the top of each page.

3. Encourage the learner to add words that he or she wants to remember how to spell and to consult this dictionary while writing.

4. Ask the learner to write a sample sentence next to the word, if necessary, as a clue to the meaning. This is especially helpful with homonyms.

    Examples: sun   The sun came up.

                  son   Mike is my son.

Suggestion

*   The spelling dictionary could also have pages for different categories of words (e.g., job application words, family names, words used in school notes, foods, number words, street sign words, or parts list for use in the learner's job).

Activity 69   A Multisensory Approach to Spelling

Purpose

To encourage the learner to use as many senses as possible when studying a word to increase the likelihood of remembering how to spell it

How

Ask the learner to do the following with each word that he or she wants to learn to spell.

1. Look at the word.

2. Read the word.

   "kitchen"

3. Note the parts that are written the way they sound.

   k i t c h e n

4. Note the parts that are not written the way they sound.

   k i t c h e n

5. Note any special points to remember.

   /c/ sound made by *k*
   silent *t*

6. Read the word again.

   "kitchen"

7. Say the letters in sequence while looking at the word. (If the word has more than one syllable, help the learner divide it into syllables and say the letters for each syllable.)

   "k-i-t-c-h" "e-n"

8. Look at the word again. Read it.

   "kitchen"

9. Close your eyes and see the word in your mind.

   kitchen

10. Spell the word aloud as you see it in your mind.

    "k-i-t-c-h-e-n"

11. Write the word without looking at a model.

12. Check to see if you are right.

    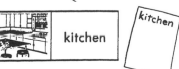

Teaching Adults: A Literacy Resource Book

Suggestion

- Neurolinguistic research shows that when people try to picture something in their minds, their eyes tend to move upward. To help a learner improve the ability to visualize and remember how a word looks, write the word on the board for study. You can also write it on a flash card that you hold above eye level.

Pulling It All Together: Lesson Planning

General Principles for Planning Lessons

There are five general principles to keep in mind as you plan your lessons:

1. Lessons should revolve around the learner's goals.

A learner can travel many different pathways to reach personal goals. Lesson planning involves working with the learner to identify which path works best and what steps need to be taken. A lesson plan is not carved in stone; it is a guide. Tutors need to remain flexible enough to change paths if the learner's needs change or if the tutor finds something that works better. Be willing to take some side trips when special needs arise.

2. Lessons should build on each other.

   Build on what the learner already knows when introducing new material. Move from the simple to the more complex.

3. Each lesson should include time for review and reinforcement.

   When you introduce a new concept, plan time in the next lesson to review and reinforce the learning with a variety of activities, such as games, puzzles, flash cards, computer software, and kinesthetic/tactile activities.

4. Each lesson should integrate all four communication tools.

   The learner should use listening, speaking, reading, and writing in every lesson.

5. The learner should learn something new in each lesson.

   Learners need to feel that they are making progress and constantly building on what they know.

The Planning Process

Planning is dynamic. It involves preparing the lesson, doing the lesson with the learner, and evaluating the results. It is not a linear process; rather, it is a series of connected loops, as one lesson leads into another, building on previous material and preparing for lessons to come.

1. Plan the lesson. In preparing each lesson plan, consider these questions:

   - What are the learning objectives? What will the learner accomplish?

   - What materials will you use?

   - What activities and teaching techniques will you use?

   - How can you integrate listening, speaking, reading, and writing in the lesson?

   - How much time will you spend on each activity?

   - How will you and the learner answer the question, "Was it a good lesson?"

2. Do the lesson.

3. Evaluate the lesson. Assess the effectiveness of the lesson by

   - talking with the learner

   - asking the learner to record thoughts in a journal or dialog journal (See Activities #59 and #60.)

   - making notes in your tutor log (See "Tutor Learning Logs" in the chapter "Evaluating Progress.")

   - writing ideas for the next lesson

Sample Lesson Plans

A learner profile of Robert and two sample lesson plans for him are shown below. The profile includes the last entry in the tutor's log. The two lesson plans are two different ways to design the next lesson. Lesson Plan 1 focuses on the skills taught in the primary instructional series. In Lesson Plan 2, the tutor and learner decide to set the series aside for the moment and focus on the learner's goal of obtaining his commercial driver's license.

Learner Profile: Robert

- Personal information

  23 years old

  Married, expecting first child

  Interests: basketball, playing cards

- Previous schooling

  Completed ninth grade

- Employment

  Warehouse worker (Heartland Printing)

- Long-term goals/needs

  Improve his reading and writing

  Become a delivery truck driver for Heartland

- Short-term objectives/needs

  Pass commercial driver's license (CDL) exam

  Find a new apartment for family

- Current tutoring information

  Five months in the program

  Meets twice a week for a total of three hours

- Primary instructional series: the *Laubach Way to Reading* series (*LWR*)

Last note in tutor's log

> 9/20/93
> Completed Lesson 11 of LWR Book 2. Introduced different spellings for /er/. Worked on basic map-reading skills he will need to make deliveries. Need to review concepts of north, south, east, and west. For homework, he will make a map of his immediate neighborhood.

Lesson Plan 1

Objectives

- be able to read the story for *LWR* Book 2, Lesson 12 fluently
- be able to recognize words with the -*ar* pattern
- be able to describe the kind of apartment he wants
- be able to find the newspaper ads for apartments in the neighborhood in which he wants to live
- be able to recognize 10 commonly used newspaper ad abbreviations (e.g., *bdrm, apt/apts, sec dep, avail immed, incl heat, refrig, full appls, central air, laund rm, off st pkg*)

Plan

Getting settled (5 minutes)

LWR Book 2, Lesson 12 (30 minutes)

- Chart, Story (duet reading), Skills Practice (sections 1, 2)

Check homework (10 minutes)

Break (5 minutes)

Short-term objective: find an apartment (30 minutes)

- List what you want in an apartment: cost, location, etc.
- Use classified ads to locate apartments in preferred location.
- Read sample ads and use flash cards to review abbreviations.

Evaluate lesson: journal entry followed by discussion (5 minutes)

Assign homework (5 minutes)

- Circle apartment ads that meet your requirements.
- Write five questions to ask the landlord.

Review objectives/materials needed for next lesson

Lesson Plan 2

Objectives

- review words with different spellings of the /er/ sound pattern
- understand the content of one section of the CDL manual
- learn six sight words from that section
- be able to use mapping to identify what you want to write

Plan

Getting settled (5 minutes)

Check homework (10 minutes)
(or do in class if not completed at home)

Review objectives (2 minutes)

Short-term objective: commercial driver's license manual (50 minutes plus 5-minute break)

- Robert uses table of contents to select section to work on.
- Discuss the topic; then read it to him.
- LEA: Robert dictates what he wants to remember about this section.
- Identify and practice reading six key sight words from LEA.
- Practice words with /er/ sound.

Writing (10 minutes)

- Map ideas for "Why I want to get my commercial driver's license."

Evaluate lesson by reviewing how well objectives were met (5 minutes)

Assign homework (3 minutes)

- Reread LEA piece.
- Write draft of paragraph using the map about getting CDL.

Review plans for next lesson (5 minutes)

The First Meeting

Tutors and learners are often anxious about the first meeting. With some planning, however, you can help make the learner and yourself more comfortable.

- Make it clear that your purpose is to help the learner learn what he or she wants and needs to know.

- Spend some time getting to know each other. Get to know the learner as an individual. Learn about the learner's life, interests, and goals. Do some initial assessment of strengths and needs. (See "Doing Your Own Assessment" in the chapter "Finding a Starting Point" for suggestions about how to do an initial assessment.)

- Plan at least one instructional activity. A language experience story can break the ice. You can also supply two or three reading selections at different levels. The learner can choose which to read (or you can read it to the learner).

- Discuss and confirm the time, date, and location of the next lesson.

- Work together to set objectives for the next lesson.

- Discuss the kinds of materials you will be using.

Evaluating Progress

The initial assessment (discussed in the chapter "Finding a Starting Point") gives you a good starting point for working with a learner. Assessment, however, is an ongoing process that helps measure progress and guides the course of instruction. Three effective tools for evaluating progress are

- a portfolio
- a tutor learning log
- a student learning log

Portfolios

Portfolios have several purposes:

- to document learning and assess progress over time
- to help the learner develop self-evaluation skills by reflecting on the learning
- to demonstrate the variety of reading and writing activities the learner has performed
- to help the tutor and the learner identify needs and plan future lessons
- (optional) to show program representatives how the learner is doing

Guidelines

There is no one right way to compile a portfolio. You can use the following suggestions to help you decide what will work for you:

- Decide what you will keep the portfolio in. This could be a three-ring binder, an accordion file, a file folder, or a box with a lid.

- Collect data early in the tutoring process so you have baseline information on the learner's starting point (e.g., initial assessment information, your observations from the first few weeks of tutoring, or first writing samples).

- Work with the learner to decide what progress you want the portfolio to measure or track.

- Together with the learner, select portfolio items that help you measure progress in selected areas and that represent all the ways the learner uses reading and writing. Make sure all items are dated so you can track change.

- Have the learner periodically add and delete materials so the portfolio reflects continued growth.

- Have the learner write or dictate the reasons for choosing certain items and how they reflect his or her literacy development. Include these explanations in the portfolio.

- Every few months, review the contents of the portfolio with the learner to assess progress; identify current needs; and help plan future goals, objectives, and activities. In addition, make notes on how the portfolio shows progress from the baseline or from the last portfolio review.

- Encourage the learner to also develop a display portfolio to demonstrate what he or she can do. The learner may choose to share this with anyone: other learners, tutors, program staff, friends, employers, etc. As with an artist's portfolio, the display portfolio consists of samples of the learner's best work.

Evaluating the Portfolio

Consider these questions as you and the learner work together to evaluate a portfolio:

Reading progress

- What has the learner read?
- What can the learner read independently?
- How is the learner using reading to meet personal needs?
- How has the learner's self-image as a reader changed?
- What reading strategies is the learner using?
- What level of comprehension is demonstrated?
- How fluent an oral reader is the learner?

- How many words can the learner write?

- How has the length of the learner's sentences changed?

- How does the learner use punctuation?

- How clearly does the learner express ideas?

- What range of writing tasks has the learner tried?

- How has the learner's self-image as a writer changed?

- How complex is the learner's writing?

- How legible is the learner's printing or handwriting?

Materials to Include in a Portfolio

Learners and tutors must work together to decide what to include in the portfolio to reflect the learner's progress. The following are some examples of what you might include:

- writing samples

- lists of books read (with brief descriptions or evaluations)

- lists of new ways learner uses reading and writing

- learner log (see "Student Learning Logs" in this chapter)

- learner's reflections on the portfolio pieces

- photocopies of selected journal or dialog journal pages (see Activities #59 and #60)

- printing and cursive writing samples

- language experience stories

- audiotapes of learner reading aloud

- checkups or periodic tests that are part of a published instructional series

- descriptions of reading strategies learner is using

- published writings

- samples of real-life materials learner has read or written (e.g., recipes, application forms, letters)

- works in progress

- lists of specialized sight word vocabulary learner has mastered

- items that show development in writing style, organization, clarity, or word choice

- samples of first and final drafts that show idea development and self-editing

- goal statements

Tutor Learning Logs

A tutor log (see example on p. 132) is an ongoing record of the tutoring process. After each lesson, the tutor makes notes about

- what the learner worked on

- what was discussed during the lesson evaluation

- what the tutor observed as the learner did the planned activities or used the materials

- the learner's strengths and needs

- ideas for future instruction

- stories or experiences the learner described that illustrate how the learner's skills are improving or the impact tutoring is having on the learner

- the tutor's thoughts about the tutoring process; how the tutor is growing and changing

The tutor then reviews these notes periodically to determine

- how the learner has improved

- what the learner needs to work on

- the types of materials or activities that seemed to work best

Tutors can choose to share some of the notes with the learner as appropriate.

Example of Tutor Log

6/6

Finishing up with *Challenger 2*. Began work on the final review chapter today. I was really thrilled to see how easily she read the vocab. words she had learned and how she could tell me basic info. about the story the words were taken from. Really impressed she retained so much of what she'd read weeks ago.

Seems to have excellent comprehension when reading, but has difficulty interpreting instructions for exercises. We usually review instructions together and if it seems she does not get the homework instructions, we go over them and do sample exercises. Seems that if she doesn't follow through with homework soon after our lesson, she gets confused about exercises and doesn't finish them. I would like to boost her confidence. Maybe I'll prepare a special sheet of instructions with a few exercises to work on together in class.

6/10

Liz's concentration was low tonight—repeatedly misread words she should not have difficulty with. Had trouble seeing the difference between *r* and *n*. When she had difficulty pronouncing a word, I asked her to sound out letters and to see if the letter was *r* or *n*. I didn't know what to do. It really seems like she can't see the difference between the two letters. Will talk to program director or another tutor to see if they have any suggestions.

6/13

Another tutor suggested creating paragraphs using short words with *r* and *n* and having Liz circle words containing one letter and underlining ones that have the other. I'm going to try to see if she will confuse the two if her task is to concentrate on seeing *r* or *n*.

Liz and Fred are planning to drive to California for vacation. I worry because they are both literacy students and there are a lot of things that can happen on a road trip to California! Not to mention the undependability of their car. Still, they're excited and enthusiastic, so Liz and I did some work and made some plans related to her trip. She wants to

- review a U.S. map

- plot out a route they might take

- set up a trip journal to keep her working on her writing skills

- select a fiction book to read on the trip

(Adapted from a tutor log kept by Cyndi Guy, The Learning Place, Syracuse, NY.)

Teaching Adults: A Literacy Resource Book

Student Learning Logs

When the learner is ready, the tutor can encourage the learner also to keep a log or journal. The learner can write about what he or she is learning and feelings about it. The learner can also write about things learned outside of tutoring. Tutors should periodically allow time in the lesson for the learner to reflect on learning and make an entry in the log. The tutor can suggest topics, such as

- what I worked on during the lesson
- what I have learned in the past two weeks
- what I think about the lesson
- what I need to work on
- ideas for future lesson activities

New Readers Press Publications

New Readers Press (NRP) develops, publishes, and distributes print, audio, video, and computer-based instructional materials in reading, writing, spelling, math, English as a second language, life skills, GED, family literacy, and workplace literacy. The items listed below are a sample of the materials available from NRP.

General Reading and Writing

ReadingWise

This eight-level comprehension-based program helps students understand what they read in documents and other nonfiction works such as newspaper articles, how-to instructions, charts and graphs, workplace documents, and first-aid instructions. Each lesson focuses on a single comprehension strategy such as

- predicting outcomes,
- separating fact from opinion,
- understanding cause and effect, and
- summarizing and paraphrasing.

The series can be used in conjunction with any core reading series or instructional approach.

The *Laubach Way to Reading* Series

This is an update of NRP's original reading series developed by Frank C. Laubach, Betty Mooney Kirk, and Robert S. Laubach. The four-book sequential skills series uses a controlled vocabulary and takes a learner from a zero reading level to approximately a fifth-grade level. Components for each level include a student skill book, a detailed teacher's manual, a correlated reader with stories using the vocabulary and sentence structures taught in that level, a checkup booklet, and a diploma.

For additional practice, learners can read *More Stories* for each level or try their hand at one of the three correlated crossword puzzle books. For learners who want to practice reading independently, NRP publishes read-along tapes for the stories in the skill books, the correlated readers, and *More Stories 1–4*.

Other supplemental materials include four *Laubach Way to English* workbooks, which provide practice in grammar and sentence structure. The *LWR Software* helps a person learn to use context clues by completing three CLOZE exercises for each lesson in the skill books. NRP also publishes the *LWR Diagnostic Inventory*, which can help place a learner in the appropriate skill book. The following is a brief list of the skills introduced in the four levels of *LWR*:

Level 1—Sounds and Names of Letters

names of letters

sound for each consonant

short vowel sounds

blending sounds to form words

printing

capital letters: purpose

numerals and number words

basic punctuation (.,“ ” !)

basic sight vocabulary

Level 2—Short Vowel Sounds

short vowel sounds

short vowel patterns

consonant blends

word parts: endings

reading fiction

understanding/comprehension

writing words and sentences

spelling

Level 3—Long Vowel Sounds

long vowel sounds

long vowel patterns

spelling of long vowel sounds

word parts: compound words, contractions

syllables

cursive writing

applying skills to real-world tasks

Level 4—Other Vowel Sounds and Consonant Spellings

other vowel sounds (e.g., *food, Paul*)

consonant sounds with more than one spelling (e.g., *fish, phone*)

word parts: prefixes, suffixes

reading nonfiction

writing paragraphs

applying skills to real-world tasks

The *Challenger Adult Reading* Series

Challenger is an eight-book series that takes a learner from second-grade to eighth-grade reading level. Developed by Corea Murphy, the series contains a variety of thought-provoking fiction and nonfiction selections that stimulate interest in reading and help learners expand their background knowledge of the culture in which they live. Detailed teacher's manuals provide guidance in lesson planning and suggestions for supplemental writing and skills reinforcement activities. The series also includes answer keys for all written exercises in the eight student books and a diploma that can be presented at the completion of each book.

NRP also publishes the *Challenger Placement Tool* to aid in determining where to start learners in this series. In addition, puzzle books for each level and separate writing books for levels 1 through 4 enable tutors to tailor instruction to the needs of each learner. The series is suitable for both one-to-one and small-group instruction.

The four correlated writing books, *Writing for Challenger 1–4,* provide additional writing practice for each lesson in the first four *Challenger* books. The writing books allow teachers to regularly integrate writing skills practice easily into their reading lessons. Because the writing books are based on the content and vocabulary of the lessons in the corresponding reading books, they reinforce comprehension of the reading selections and vocabulary building while developing writing and thinking skills.

Voyager: Reading and Writing for Today's Adults

Voyager: Reading and Writing for Today's Adults is a nine-level series that offers a rich mixture of authentic reading selections and writing assignments and combines a contemporary theme-based approach with the proven elements from traditional direct instruction.

- Reading, writing, listening, speaking, and thinking skills are integrated in every lesson.

- Learning Goals at the beginning of every lesson affirm learners' need to understand what they're going to learn and why.

- Early books combine phonics with reading comprehension; later books emphasize comprehension at literal, inferential, and applied levels.

- Instruction in the writing process is combined with instruction in spelling, capitalization, punctuation, grammar, usage, and sentence structure.

- The series integrates all the tools needed for assessment.

Phonics

Focus on Phonics

This four-level series teaches phonics principles in the same order they are introduced in the *Laubach Way to Reading* series. Each student book is accompanied by a detailed teacher's edition. The series can provide extra practice for an *LWR* learner or can be used to teach phonics to other learners. It also provides excellent spelling practice. Author: Gail V. Rice.

- *Focus on Phonics-1:* Sounds and Names of Letters
- *Focus on Phonics-2a:* Short Vowel Sounds
- *Focus on Phonics-2b:* Consonant Blends
- *Focus on Phonics-3:* Long Vowel Sounds
- *Focus on Phonics-4:* Other Vowel Sounds and Consonant Spellings

Spelling

Patterns in Spelling

This four-book program is for adults and older teens who are reading at level 3 or higher. It teaches spelling by stressing patterns regularly found in English words. The series includes a diagnostic/placement test, and each level has a separate teacher's edition and diploma. Authors: Tim Brown and Deborah F. Knight.

- Book 1: Patterns with Short Vowels
- Book 2: Patterns with Long Vowels
- Book 3: Patterns with Consonant Blends and Digraphs
- Book 4: Patterns with Other Vowel Sounds

Structures in Spelling

Structures in Spelling teaches the spelling of words containing prefixes, roots, and suffixes. It can be used independently with advanced learners or with learners who need further work on the skills developed in *Patterns in Spelling*. Includes a teacher's edition. Authors: Tim Brown and Deborah F. Knight.

Writing

The Laubach Way to Cursive Writing

This book uses an easy-to-follow dot and arrow system. Learners practice writing meaningful words and phrases on checks, notes, personal letters, and envelopes. It is designed to be used independently or in conjunction with *Skill Book 3* of the *Laubach Way to Reading* series. Includes a teacher's guide. Author: Kay Koschnick.

Writing Me!

Writing Me! encourages beginning writers to write about themselves and the things that are important to them. It includes work on language experience, sentence combining, peer evaluation, and values clarification. Author: Tana Reiff.

Writing It Down

This text helps adults learn to use writing as a communication tool. It focuses on everyday writing tasks, such as application forms, grocery and other lists, absence notes and permission slips, and personal letters. Written by the staff of the Women's Program of the Lutheran Settlement House in Philadelphia.

Math

Math Sense

Math Sense is a comprehensive math series that helps adults to overcome math anxiety, discover math as interesting and purposeful, and develop solid number sense and problem-solving skills within the context of real-life and workplace experiences. It combines the best elements of traditional skill development with empowerment-based learning and integrates computation, calculator work, estimation and mental math into each lesson. *Smart Solutions (Math Sense)* is organized around four key strands: skills, problem solving, tools, and applications. There are four student books: *Whole Numbers and Money; Decimals, Fractions, Ratios and Percents; Measurement and Data Analysis;* and *Algebra and Geometry.* In addition, the *Comprehensive Math Review* book summarizes all key skills and is excellent for GED preparation, a brush-up course, or as a means of identifying problem areas.

Breakthrough to Math

Breakthrough to Math is a four-level series designed for adults who have had little or no success with standard math programs. It includes detailed diagnostic and placement tools. Editor: Ann K. U. Tussing.

- Level 1: Basic Skills with Whole Number (six books)
- Level 2: Fractions, Decimals, and Percents (six books)
- Level 3: Algebra (five books)
- Level 4: Geometry (three books)

Learning Styles

Help Yourself: How to Take Advantage of Your Learning Styles

This reference is for learners and tutors who want to better understand learning styles and their practical applications. Includes a "learning styles inventory." Author: Gail M. Sonbuchner.

Newspapers

News for You

This weekly newspaper provides ESL students and other adult learners with news that is easy to read and understand. It covers international and national current events and includes a wide range of feature articles. Stories are written at two reading levels: 2–3 and 4–6. A Teacher's Guide, included with every issue, provides reproducible exercises, activities, and discussion question for every story.

For more information about these and other NRP publications,
call (800) 448-8878 to request a free catalog or visit the online catalog at
www.newreaderspress.com.

Sample Learner Goals

The checklist on pp. 143–146 includes some of the goals of new readers in adult literacy programs. Tutors and learners can use the checklist to help them establish their own goals. There are 10 general categories:

- general skills
- transportation
- money
- jobs
- government/law
- health
- food
- children
- recreation
- religion

A good place to begin is by asking learners which categories they would like to review. Tutors can assist learners in reading these sections if necessary and then ask the learners to indicate how each column should be checked. Tutors should encourage learners to add other goals that are important to the learners.

If the learner identifies a specific goal, the tutor should take some time to find out more about the learner's interest or needs. For example, if the learner wants to read a newspaper, what parts are of greatest interest? If the learner wants to be able to write letters, what is the purpose and who is the audience?

	I do it well enough	I want to work on it	I don't need to work on this now

General Skills

Write my name, address, and telephone number			
Write other people's names, addresses, and telephone numbers			
Tell time			
Read a calendar			
Write down appointments			
Use a telephone book			
Read street signs			
Read store names and signs			
Read or write a letter or note			
Read a newspaper			
Read a magazine			
Read a book			
Use a dictionary			
Other:			

Transportation

Read bus or train schedules			
Read traffic signs			
Read a driver's manual			
Read maps			
Read a car maintenance/repair manual			
Other:			

	I do it well enough	I want to work on it	I don't need to work on this now

Money

Read pricing labels in stores

Write checks or money orders

Read a bank statement

Read and pay bills

Fill out an application for a credit card

Fill out public assistance forms

Fill out unemployment forms

Fill out tax forms

Other:

Jobs

Read job ads

Fill out a job application

Read job-related manuals/forms

Write a résumé

Read information on paychecks

Read charts, graphs, or diagrams

Read contracts

Fill out order forms

Make lists

Write reports

Other:

Appendix B

	I do it well enough	I want to work on it	I don't need to work on this now

Government/Law

Read an election ballot

Read leases

Read legal documents/forms

Read about government or history

Other:

Health

Read a thermometer

Read labels/directions on medicine bottles

Read warning/poison labels

Read about what to do for injuries or sickness

Fill out medical or dental insurance forms

Read about staying healthy

Read about pregnancy and childbirth

Read about AIDS or other diseases/health problems

Other:

Food

Write a shopping list

Read grocery ads

Read coupons

Read food labels

Read recipes

Read menus

Other:

	I do it well enough	I want to work on it	I don't need to work on this now

Children

Read books to children

Read school notices and reports

Fill out school forms

Write notes to the school

Write a medical history/record of shots

Read about child care

Other:

Recreation

Read a TV or radio program schedule

Read a movie schedule/movie reviews

Read words to songs

Read notices or newsletters about community activities

Read directions or rules for playing games

Fill out an application for a library card

Other:

Religion

Read church bulletins

Read the Bible or other religious materials

Read aloud during religious services

Other:

Sample Criteria for Evaluating Materials

People use many different criteria when choosing instructional materials for beginning readers. The list below includes some of the criteria you might consider as you try to select appropriate materials for a specific learner. Which criteria you decide to use will also depend on the type of materials and their purpose (to build or reinforce skills, to present information, or to entertain).

As you work together, encourage the learner to evaluate the materials or suggest others. Remember that the real test of the effectiveness of material is not whether it meets the criteria presented here, but whether it meets the needs of the learner.

Print Materials for the Learner

Content (Text and Illustrations)

- Is relevant to the learner's
  - goals
  - needs
  - interests
  - experiences
  - values
  - culture
- Is adult-oriented
- Helps build positive self-image in the learner
- Doesn't assume previous knowledge or experience that the learner doesn't have

- Doesn't promote stereotypes of
  - racial, ethnic, or cultural groups
  - people from specific states or regions of the country
  - men or women
  - age groups
  - people with specific health conditions or disabilities
  - economic groups
- Is free from bias (cultural, religious, ethnic, racial, class, sexual, etc.)
- Contains accurate, up-to-date information
- Presents information in a logical sequence, building from the known to the unknown
- Is written at an appropriate reading level if the learner will use it independently
- Contains enjoyable reading selections that motivate the learner to read more
- Uses a writing style appropriate for the learner
- Contains graphics (photos, illustrations, charts) that enhance the text and do not confuse or distract the learner
- Other:

Additional Content Criteria for Published Instructional Materials

- Contains clear explanations of any new skills or concepts
- Can be adapted to accommodate differences in individual learners
- Provides adequate opportunity for practicing and reinforcing skills
- Provides feedback to the learner on how he or she is doing
- Encourages the learner to apply the skills and information in real-life contexts
- When appropriate, contains clear directions and adequate support for the tutor or teacher
- Other:

Format

- Is adult in appearance
- Has appropriate typeface and type size

- Has appropriate line length (not too short or too long) for the type size
- Has adequate spacing between the lines of type
- Has spacing between words that is not distracting (if the lines of type are justified)
- Uses color, if any, to enhance readability (In general, type should be black on white paper for greatest contrast and ease of reading.)
- Appears inviting and easy to read
  - graphics or subheads to break up solid text
  - adequate use of white space
- Has a layout that enhances readability and does not confuse the reader
- Has clear graphics (pictures, charts, illustrations) that are near the relevant text
- Has cover, photos, and illustrations that are appropriate for the learner
- Has paper that
  - is heavy enough so type (or handwriting, if it is a workbook) doesn't show through from other side of page
  - is free from glare
- Other:

Cost

- Fits within the budget
- Is appropriate for the type of material and how it will be used

Computer Software for the Learner

Many of the above criteria can also be used to evaluate instructional software. Some other characteristics to look for in software include the following:

- Is compatible with the available hardware
- Allows user to enter and exit the program with ease
- Is easy to learn (user-friendly) for a person unfamiliar with computers or keyboarding skills
- Has clear learning objectives
- Has on-screen directions that are clear and can be read by the learner
- Has a way to let the learner check answers without the tutor's assistance

- If appropriate, has an authoring system that allows the tutor to tailor instruction to individual needs

- Has text, graphics, and music (if any) that are adult-oriented

- Requires active learner participation

- Includes sufficient practice of any new concept being taught

- Has a way to record where the learner leaves off and an easy way for the learner to get back to that place

- Provides feedback to the learner and the tutor on how well the learner is doing and what areas need more work

- Allows time for reflection and response

- Allows the learner to control the rate and sequence of the program

- Has audio components (if any) that are easy to understand

- Allows users to make a backup copy in case anything happens to the original

- If desired, has a management or record-keeping system to track learner progress

- Has a strong support component (i.e., the publisher will troubleshoot or answer questions if you have difficulty)

- Other:

Teacher's Guides

Many of the same criteria used for evaluating learner materials also apply to teacher's guides. In addition, you should consider the following:

- Contains clear directions

- Provides an adequate level of support to the teacher or tutor

- Is designed so that the teacher can find information quickly and easily

- Contains directions for how to place a learner in the materials

- Describes how to adapt the materials to meet individual needs

- Includes a way to check the learner's progress and needs

300 Most Frequently Used Words

The following 300 words make up 65 percent of all written material.
The words are listed in their order of frequency.

1. the	23. this	45. which	67. into
2. of	24. have	46. she	68. time
3. and	25. from	47. do	69. has
4. a	26. or	48. how	70. look
5. to	27. one	49. their	71. two
6. in	28. had	50. if	72. more
7. is	29. by	51. will	73. write
8. you	30. words	52. up	74. go
9. that	31. but	53. other	75. see
10. it	32. not	54. about	76. number
11. he	33. what	55. out	77. no
12. was	34. all	56. many	78. way
13. for	35. were	57. then	79. could
14. on	36. we	58. them	80. people
15. are	37. when	59. these	81. my
16. as	38. your	60. so	82. than
17. with	39. can	61. some	83. first
18. his	40. said	62. her	84. water
19. they	41. there	63. would	85. been
20. I	42. use	64. make	86. called
21. at	43. an	65. like	87. who
22. be	44. each	66. him	88. oil

89. its	122. good	155. another	188. house
90. now	123. sentence	156. well	189. point
91. find	124. man	157. large	190. page
92. long	125. think	158. must	191. letters
93. down	126. say	159. big	192. mother
94. day	127. great	160. even	193. answer
95. did	128. where	161. such	194. found
96. get	129. help	162. because	195. study
97. come	130. through	163. turned	196. still
98. made	131. much	164. here	197. learn
99. may	132. before	165. why	198. should
100. part	133. line	166. asked	199. American
101. over	134. right	167. went	200. world
102. new	135. too	168. men	201. high
103. sound	136. means	169. read	202. every
104. take	137. old	170. need	203. near
105. only	138. any	171. land	204. add
106. little	139. same	172. different	205. food
107. work	140. tell	173. home	206. between
108. know	141. boy	174. us	207. own
109. place	142. following	175. move	208. below
110. years	143. came	176. try	209. country
111. live	144. want	177. kind	210. plants
112. me	145. show	178. hand	211. last
113. back	146. also	179. picture	212. school
114. give	147. around	180. again	213. father
115. most	148. form	181. change	214. keep
116. very	149. three	182. off	215. trees
117. after	150. small	183. play	216. never
118. things	151. set	184. spell	217. started
119. our	152. put	185. air	218. city
120. just	153. end	186. away	219. earth
121. name	154. does	187. animals	220. eyes

221. light	241. life	261. sea	281. watch
222. thought	242. always	262. began	282. far
223. head	243. those	263. grow	283. Indians
224. under	244. both	264. took	284. really
225. story	245. paper	265. river	285. almost
226. saw	246. together	266. four	286. let
227. left	247. got	267. carry	287. above
228. don't	248. group	268. state	288. girl
229. few	249. often	269. once	289. sometimes
230. while	250. run	270. book	290. mountains
231. along	251. important	271. hear	291. cut
232. might	252. until	272. stop	292. young
233. close	253. children	273. without	293. talk
234. something	254. side	274. second	294. soon
235. seemed	255. feet	275. later	295. list
236. next	256. car	276. miss	296. song
237. hard	257. miles	277. idea	297. being
238. open	258. night	278. enough	298. leave
239. example	259. walked	279. eat	299. family
240. beginning	260. white	280. face	300. it's

Taken from Elizabeth Sakiey and Edward Fry, *3000 Instant Words,* rev. ed., Jamestown Publishers, 1984.

Social Sight Words

A

Adults Only

Ask Attendant for Key

B

Beware

Beware of the Dog

Bus Stop

C

Caution

Closed

Condemned

D

Danger

Dentist

Doctor (Dr.)

Do Not Cross

Do Not Enter

Do Not Refreeze

Don't Walk

Down

E

Elevator

Emergency Exit

Employees Only

Entrance

Exit

Exit Only

F

Fire Escape

Fire Extinguisher

First Aid

Fragile

G

Gentlemen

H

Handle with Care

Hands Off

Help

High Voltage

I

In

Inflammable

Information

Instructions

K

Keep Away

Keep Closed at All Times

Keep Off (the Grass)

Keep Out

L

Ladies

Last Chance for Gas

Listen

Live Wires

Look

M

Men

Men Working

N

Next Window

No Admittance

No Checks Cashed

No Credit

No Credit Cards Accepted

No Dogs Allowed

No Dumping

No Fires

No Fishing

No Hunting

No Loitering

No Minors

No Smoking

No Smoking Area

No Spitting

No Swimming

No Trespassing

Nurse

O

Office

Open

Out

Out of Order

P

Pedestrians Prohibited

Police Station

Post No Bills

Post Office

Private

Private Property

Pull

Push

R

Rest Rooms

S

Smoking Prohibited

Step Down

Stop

T

This End Up

This Side Up

U

Use Before (Date)

Use Other Door

V

Violators Will Be Prosecuted

W

Walk

Wanted

Warning

Watch Your Step

Wet Paint

Women

Taken from the *Laubach Way to Reading Tutor Workshop Handbook.*

How to Make Speech Sounds

Adult learners need to be able to use the sounds of letters as one tool to help them recognize printed words. Being able to identify the sounds in a word they hear will also help learners spell the word.

Tutors and teachers can use the chart on pp. 157–161 for several purposes:

- To check which sounds the learner already knows and which ones to work on, you can do one of the following:

  - Cover everything on the page except the first column and ask the learner to make the sound for each letter or letter combination as you point to it.

  - Point to the word in the second column. Ask the learner to read it (or read it yourself), and then ask the learner to make the sound for the letter(s) in bold type. This will not tell you if the learner knows the sound in isolation, but it will tell you if he or she has the concept of sounds. Note that you can also substitute words of your own choosing for those in column 2.

- To help describe how a sound is made (if the learner is having difficulty producing it)

- As a reference to the variety of ways that a sound can be spelled

The following codes are used in column 4 to describe the sounds in the chart:

    v = voiced (the vocal cords vibrate)

    un = unvoiced (the vocal cords do not vibrate)

    c = continuant (sound can be continued as long as the speaker has breath)

    s = stop (sound can't be continued)

    n = nasal (sound comes through the nose)

Consonant Sounds

Sound	As In	Other Spellings	Code	Mouth Position
b	bird		v s	Stop air with lips together; open with small puff of breath. Voiced equivalent of /p/.
c	cup	kitchen kick Chris	un s	Tongue tip down, back of tongue touching lower teeth. Stop air with hump or arch of the tongue and emit breath from back of throat. Unvoiced equivalent of /g/.
d	dish		v s	Lips and teeth slightly parted. Stop air with tongue tip touching roof of mouth just behind upper teeth. Tongue is dropped as breath is expelled. Voiced equivalent of /t/.
f	fish	phone tough	un c	Lower lip touching upper teeth lightly. Unvoiced equivalent of /v/.
g	girl		v s	Tongue tip down, touching back of lower teeth. Stop air with hump or arch of the tongue and emit breath from back of throat. Voiced equivalent of /k/ or /c/ above.
h	hand		un c	Has no position of its own. Position the tongue for the vowel following it and give breath sound.
j	jumping	gentle ginger gym judge	v	A combination of /d/ and /zh/. Lips forward. Start with tongue tip up. Lower as breath is expelled. Voiced equivalent of /ch/.
k	kitchen	cup kick Chris	un s	Same as /c/ above.
l	leg		v c	Tongue tip touches just behind the upper teeth. Air comes out along the side(s) of the tongue.
m	man		v n c	Lips together. It is made with the same lip position as /b/ and /p/, but /b/ and /p/ are stops.

Sound	As In	Other Spellings	Code	Mouth Position
n	**n**eck	**kn**ock **gn**aw	v n c	Lips and teeth slightly parted. Tongue tip touching roof of mouth just behind upper teeth. Lower surface of tongue shows. Tongue touches the gum ridge with position like /t/ and /d/, but /t/ and /d/ are stops.
p	**p**an		un s	Stop air with lips together; open with big puff of breath. Unvoiced equivalent of /b/.
qu	**qu**arter		un	Teach as /kw/. Lips rounded like *oo* as in *room*.
r	**r**iver	**wr**ap	v c	Tongue tip down. Lips forward and almost squared. Round lips before voicing.
s	**s**nake	**c**ent **c**ity bi**c**ycle	un c	Teeth close but not touching. Tongue tip down. Unvoiced equivalent of /z/.
t	**t**ent		un s	Lips and teeth slightly parted. Stop air with tongue tip up touching roof of mouth just behind upper teeth. Lower surface of tongue shows. Tongue is dropped as breath is expelled. Unvoiced equivalent of /d/.
v	**v**alley		v c	Lower lip touching upper teeth lightly. Voiced equivalent of /f/.
w	**w**oman		v c	Lips forward and rounded, with "one-finger" opening, as with *oo* in *room*.
x	bo**x**	loo**ks** ki**cks**	un	Teach as /ks/.
y	**y**ells		v c	Lips drawn back, teeth close together, as with /ee/.
z	**z**ipper	hi**s** teache**s**	v c	Teeth close but not touching. Tongue tip down. Voiced equivalent of /s/.

Sound	As In	Other Spellings	Code	Mouth Position
ch	**ch**ildren	ki**tch**en	un	A combination of /t/ and /sh/. Lips forward. Start with tongue tip up; lower as breath is expelled. Unvoiced equivalent of /j/. A consonant digraph.
ng	ri**ng**		v n c	Tongue tip down behind lower teeth. Hump or arch tongue. Nasal equivalent of /k/ or /g/. A consonant digraph.
sh	**sh**op	**Ch**icago	un c	Lips forward and squared. Teeth close but not touching. Tongue down. Tongue has wider groove than in /s/ sound. Unvoiced equivalent of /zh/ as in *measure.* A consonant digraph.
s	mea**s**ure	televi**s**ion	v c	/zh/. Voiced equivalent of /sh/.
th	**th**e		v c	Tongue touches both upper and lower teeth. Voiced equivalent of /th/ below. A consonant digraph.
th	**th**anks		un c	Tongue touches both upper and lower teeth. Unvoiced equivalent of /th/ above. A consonant digraph.
wh	**wh**istle		un c	Teach as /hw/. A consonant digraph.

Short Vowel Sounds

Sound	As In	Other Spellings	Code	Mouth Position
a	apple		v c	Wide jaw opening. Tongue down.
e	Ed	head	v c	Lips and teeth slightly closer together than for /a/.
i	in	city	v c	Lips and teeth slightly closer together than for /e/.
o	olive		v c	Wide jaw opening. Prolong the sound.
u	up		v c	Medium jaw opening. Relaxed lips. Prolong slightly.

Long Vowel Sounds

Sound	As In	Other Spellings	Code	Mouth Position
a	ate	paint day paper	v c	Teeth about a half inch apart. Hold twice as long as /ē/. Tongue down.
e	three	eat we key Pete	v c	Lips drawn back, teeth close together. Hold twice as long as /ī/.
i	five	night spy tie I	v c	Jaw wide apart at start, then move to a narrower opening.
o	nose	boat snow go	v c	Lips forward and rounded, with a "two-finger wide" opening.
u	use	pupil few argue	v c	Teach as /ee/ plus *oo* as in *room*.

Appendix F

Other Vowel Sounds

Sound	As In	Other Spellings	Code	Mouth Position
a	all	awn Paul caught bought	v c	Lips forward, wide jaw opening. A "three-finger" opening.
ar	arms		v c	Teach according to person's local pronunciation.
oi	oil	boy	v c	Combination of /aw/ and /i/. Start with lips forward for /aw/, then draw back for /i/.
oo	food	June blue chew	v c	Lips forward and rounded, with a "one-finger" opening. Prolong the sound.
oo	book	would	v c	Lips forward, almost squared.
or	horn	floor more	v c	Lips forward with a "three-finger wide" opening.
ou	out	town	v c	Combination of /o/ plus *oo* as in *room*. Start with wide jaw opening, move lips forward with a small opening.
ur	burn	her girl	v c	Tongue tip down. Lips forward, almost squared, more relaxed than for /r/.

Common Phonics Elements and Principles in English

Consonants

Consonant Letters That Represent One Sound

b	bed	k	kite	qu	queen	y	you
d	dime	l	lake	r	rope	z	zoo
f	feet	m	man	t	ten		
h	hat	n	name	v	vase		
j	job	p	pen	w	woman		

Consonant Letters with More Than One Sound

s   sun, rose   Note: *s* can sound like /s/ or /z/

x   six, example, xylophone   *x* can sound like /ks/, /gz/, or /z/

c   can, cop, cup   Rule: *c* followed by *a, o,* or *u* sounds like /k/

     cent, city, icy   *c* followed by *e, i,* or *y* sounds like /s/

g   gas, got, gum   Rule: *g* followed by *a, o,* or *u* sounds like /g/

     ginger, germ, gym   *g* followed by *e, i,* or *y* can sound like /j/

     get, give, fogy   *g* followed by *e, i,* or *y* can also sound like /g/

gu   guard, guess, guilt, guy   Rule: *gu* followed by a vowel sounds like /g/

     The *u* is usually silent.

Consonant Blends

Consonant blends are two or three consonants (or a consonant and digraph) that commonly occur together. Each sound can be heard.

Initial Blends

bl	blue	sk	skate
br	bride	sl	sleep
chr	Christmas	sm	smart
cl	clock	sn	snow
cr	cry	sp	spoon
dr	drop	spl	split
fl	flame	spr	spring
fr	friend	squ	square
gl	glass	st	step
gr	groom	str	street
pl	plate	sw	swim
pr	price	thr	throw
sc	scar	tr	track
sch	school	tw	twin
scr	scream		
shr	shrunk		

Final Blends

ct	act	rb	curb
ft	left	rce	force
ld	gold	rd	card
lf	self	rf	scarf
lk	milk	rk	bark
lm	film	rl	girl
lp	help	rm	farm
lt	melt	rn	corn
mp	lamp	rp	burp
nce	chance	rse	course
nch	lunch	rt	smart
nd	hand	sk	ask
nge	range	sp	clasp
nse	sense	st	last
nt	front	xt	next
pt	kept		

Consonant Digraphs

Consonant digraphs are two consonants that represent one sound.

ch	chair, machine, Christmas	sh	she
ng	ring	th	thing, the
nk	bank	wh	whale, who
ph	phone		

Silent Consonant Combinations

These are common consonant combinations that contain one or more silent letters. Hyphens indicate initial or final combinations.

-ck	clock	-lk	talk	sc-	scent
gh	high, rough, ghost	-lm	calm	-tch	catch
-ght	sight, thought	-mb	climb	wr-	wrong
gn	sign, gnat	-mn	autumn		
kn-	know	rh-	rhyme		

Vowels

Vowel Letters and the Sounds They Represent

Each vowel letter represents several vowel sounds. The most common sounds are represented in the words listed below. All vowels can represent the schwa sound in unstressed syllables. The schwa is represented in many dictionaries by the symbol /ə/.

	Short Sound	Long Sound	Other Sounds	Schwa Sound
a	man	name	all, father, water	about
e	bed	me	cafe	open
i	six	time	ski	April
o	job	go	son, do, dog	second
u	but	rule, fuse	put	awful
y	gym	fly	any	

Vowel Combinations and the Sounds They Represent

Listed below are common vowel digraphs or vowel-consonant combinations. Many of these combinations produce long vowel sounds. If a combination represents more than one sound, a key word is given for each common sound.

Long Vowel Sounds

ai	rain	ie	field, pie
ay	day	igh	high
ea	meat, great	ind	find
ee	feet	oa	soap
ei	either, vein	oe	toe
eigh	eight	oo	food
eu	feud	ue	due
ew	blew, few	ui	fruit
ey	key, they		

Other Vowel Sounds

ai	against	oo	book, blood
au	auto	ou	you, country, out, soul, could
aw	saw		
augh	taught, laugh	ough	though, thought, through, enough, bough, cough
ea	head		
oi	boil	ow	own, town
oy	boy	ui	build

R-Controlled and L-Controlled Vowels

When vowels are followed by *r* or *l,* the pronunciation of the vowel is usually affected.

air	fair	err	berry	urr	purr
ar	car, dollar, warm	ir	girl	al	pal, bald
arr	carry	irr	mirror	all	ball
are	care	oar	roar	ild	mild
ear	ear, earth, bear	oor	door	ol	old, roll, solve, doll
eer	deer	or	horse, word, color	ull	full, dull
er	very, her	our	hour, four, journal		
ere	here, were, there	ur	fur, fury		

Other Vowel-Consonant Combinations and the Sounds They Represent

-dge	badge	-ci-	magician, social
-ed	hated, rubbed, fixed	-si-	session, television, Asian
-gue	league	-ti-	caution, question, initial
-que	antique	su	sugar, measure
-stle	whistle	-tu-	picture

Common Syllable Patterns in English

Some patterns of letters in syllables signal short vowel sounds. Others usually produce long vowel sounds. Recognizing the common short- and long-vowel syllable
patterns can aid in decoding and spelling unknown words. It is usually the letter or
letters that follow a vowel that determine pronunciation.

Key: V = any vowel

C = any consonant

(C) = may or may not be a consonant

Syllables That Usually Produce Short Vowel Sounds

Closed syllables (syllables that end with one or more consonants)

VC: at, Ed, is, on, up

CVC: (also called 1-1-1 syllables) had, let, did, lot, but

CVCC: hand, less, with, lock, bump

Exceptions: find, child, high, sign, old, poll, bolt, most

Syllables That Usually Produce Long Vowel Sounds

VCe: (silent *e* syllables) name, eve, time, hope, rule

VV(C): (double vowel syllables) paid, need, meat, die, boat, due, food

(C)V: (open syllables) ta/ble, fe/male, bi/cycle, go, o/pen

Exceptions: Many unaccented open syllables: a/muse, to/day

A Syllable That Usually Produces the Schwa

Cle: (a consonant followed by *le*) table /tā/bəl/, gentle /gĕn/təl/

Rules for Adding Endings

The Doubling Rules

1. If a word has one syllable, one vowel, and one final consonant, double the final consonant before adding an ending that starts with a vowel. Do not double a final *w* or *x*. (This is also called the 1-1-1 Rule.)

   Examples: hop + ed = hopped
               run + ing = running
               but
               fix + ed = fixed
               row + ing = rowing

166

2. If a word has more than one syllable, double the final consonant if the last syllable has one vowel, one final consonant, is accented, and the ending starts with a vowel.

   Examples: forgót + en = forgotten

   begín + ing = beginning

   but

   óffer + ing = offering

The Silent *e* Rule

If a word ends in silent *e,* drop the final *e* before adding an ending that starts with a vowel.

   Example: joke + ing = joking

   secure + ity = security

The *y* to *i* Conversion

If a word ends in a consonant plus *y* (Cy), change the *y* to *i* before adding an ending, unless the ending starts with *i.* Note that this rule does not apply when a vowel precedes the *y.*

   Examples: lucky + er = luckier

   happy + ness = happiness

   but

   cry + ing = crying

Rules for Pronouncing the Endings

Endings *-ed* and *-d*

1. Pronounce as /d/ if preceded by a vowel sound or the voiced consonant sounds /b/, /g/, /j/, /l/, /m/, /n/, /ng/, /th/, /v/, /z/, /zh/, or /r/.

   Examples: tried   rained

   robbed   hanged

   tagged   bathed

   raged   moved

   mailed   razed

   tamed   starred

But: Some words that end in the sounds /l/, /m/, and /n/ can add either -*ed* or -*t*. Note that adding -*t* might change the sound of the root word.

Examples: spelled/spelt, dreamed/dreamt, burned/burnt

2. Pronounce as /ed/ if preceded by the sound /d/ or /t/.

Examples: kidded   posted

3. Pronounce as /t/ if preceded by the unvoiced consonant sounds /ch/, /f/, /k/, /p/, /s/, /sh/, or /th/.

Examples: reached   tapped
           stuffed   kissed
           coughed   cashed
           picked   toothed

Ending -*s*

1. Pronounce as /z/ if preceded by a vowel sound or a voiced consonant sound.

Examples: fleas   ribs
           cans   saves

2. Pronounce as /s/ if preceded by an unvoiced consonant sound.

Examples: packs
           laughs
           eats

Ending -*es*

1. Pronounce as /z/ if preceded by a vowel sound or a voiced consonant sound.

Examples: cries, calves

2. Pronounce as /iz/ if preceded by an unvoiced consonant sound.

Examples: benches   fishes
           kisses   fixes

Sample Word Patterns

For suggestions about how to teach word patterns as a word recognition strategy, see Activity #39. The list below is a sampling of some of the word patterns in English with examples of one-syllable words that contain those patterns. When teaching patterns, be careful not to mix words that have similar spellings but different sounds *(brown, blown)*.

a	**ad**	**age**	**ain**	**ale**
	bad	cage	gain	male
ab	glad	page	pain	pale
cab	had	rage	rain	sale
gab	lad	stage	stain	scale
grab	mad	wage	train	tale
stab				
tab	**ade**	**aid**	**air**	**all**
	grade	braid	chair	ball
ace	made	laid	fair	call
face	shade	maid	hair	fall
grace	trade	paid	pair	small
lace	wade	raid	stair	tall
place				
trace	**ag**	**ail**	**ake**	**am**
	bag	fail	bake	ham
ack	drag	mail	brake	jam
back	flag	pail	cake	Pam
black	rag	sail	shake	ram
crack	tag	trail	take	swam
pack				
track				

ame
blame
came
flame
name
same

an
bran
can
Dan
man
pan

and
band
hand
land
sand
stand

ane
cane
Jane
lane
plane
sane

ank
bank
crank
clank
sank
tank

ap
clap
lap
map
nap
snap

ape
cape
drape
grape
scrape
shape

are
care
fare
flare
rare
share

ash
bash
cash
dash
flash
mash

ass
bass
brass
class
glass
grass

ast
blast
cast
fast
last
past

at
bat
cat
chat
hat
that

atch
hatch
latch
match
patch
scratch

ate
fate
gate
late
plate
state

ave
brave
cave
gave
grave
save

ay
day
pay
play
say
stay

aze
blaze
daze
gaze
haze
maze

e

each
bleach
peach
preach
reach
teach

eak
creak
leak
sneak
speak
weak

eal
deal
heal
meal
real
steal

eam
beam
cream
dream
scream
team

ean
bean
clean
Jean
lean
mean

ear
clear
fear
hear
near
year

eat
beat
cheat
heat
meat
wheat

eck
check
deck
neck
peck
speck

ed
bed
Fred
red
shed
wed

eed
bleed
feed
greed
need
weed

eek
cheek
creek
Greek
peek
week

eel

feel
heel
kneel
steel
wheel

een

green
queen
screen
seen
teen

eep

creep
deep
jeep
keep
sleep

eet

beet
feet
greet
meet
sweet

ell

bell
fell
sell
spell
tell

en

den
hen
men
pen
ten

end

bend
mend
send
tend
trend

ent

bent
cent
rent
sent
went

ess

dress
guess
less
mess
press

est

best
nest
pest
test
west

et

bet
get
met
pet
set

i

ice

mice
nice
price
rice
twice

ick

chick
pick
sick
thick
tick

id

bid
did
hid
kid
skid

ide

bride
hide
pride
ride
slide

ift

drift
gift
lift
shift
sift

ig

big
dig
pig
rig
wig

ike

bike
hike
like
Mike
strike

ile

file
mile
pile
smile
while

ill

bill
fill
hill
spill
still

im

brim
dim
him
Jim
rim

ime

crime
dime
grime
slime
time

in

chin
fin
pin
sin
tin

ind

bind
blind
find
kind
mind

ine

fine
line
mine
shine
spine

ing

bring
king
ring
sing
sting

ink

blink
drink
pink
sink
wink

ip

chip
dip
hip
lip
trip

ipe

gripe
ripe
stripe
swipe
wipe

ire

fire
hire
sire
tire
wire

iss

bliss
hiss
kiss
miss
Swiss

it

bit
fit
grit
hit
sit

itch

ditch
glitch
pitch
stitch
witch

ite

bite
kite
quite
white
write

o

oat

boat
coat
float
gloat
throat

ob

Bob
cob
job
mob
rob

ock

block
clock
lock
rock
sock

od

God
nod
pod
rod
sod

og

bog
fog
hog
log
smog

oke

broke
joke
poke
smoke
spoke

old

cold
gold
hold
scold
sold

ole

hole
mole
role
stole
whole

one

bone
lone
phone
stone
zone

ool

cool
fool
school
spool
tool

oom

boom
bloom
doom
gloom
room

oon

croon
loon
moon
noon
soon

oop

coop
droop
hoop
scoop
stoop

oot

boot
hoot
loot
root
shoot

op

chop
cop
hop
mop
stop

ope

cope
hope
rope
scope
slope

ore

chore
core
more
shore
store

ose

chose
close
hose
nose
those

oss

boss
cross
loss
moss
toss

ot

got
hot
knot
lot
spot

ought

bought
brought
fought
sought
thought

ound

found
mound
pound
round
sound

172

owl	u	ug	un	unt
fowl		bug	bun	bunt
growl	**ub**	drug	fun	hunt
howl	cub	dug	gun	punt
prowl	hub	jug	run	runt
scowl	rub	snug	sun	stunt
	stub			
own	tub	**ull**	**unch**	**ush**
blown		dull	bunch	blush
flown	**uck**	gull	crunch	gush
grown	buck	lull	lunch	hush
shown	duck	mull	munch	mush
thrown	luck	skull	punch	rush
	struck			
own	truck	**um**	**ung**	**ut**
brown		bum	hung	but
clown	**ud**	chum	lung	cut
crown	bud	gum	rung	hut
down	cud	hum	stung	nut
frown	dud	sum	sung	shut
	mud			
	stud	**ump**	**unk**	
		bump	chunk	
	uff	clump	drunk	
	bluff	dump	dunk	
	cuff	jump	junk	
	huff	lump	sunk	
	puff			
	stuff			

Adapted from Tim Brown and Deborah F. Knight, *Patterns in Spelling,* New Readers Press, 1990.

Prefixes and Suffixes

Prefixes

a-
without; on, in; in a state of

ad-, ac-, af-, al-, ap-, as-, at-
toward, to, near, or in

anti-
against, opposing

auto-, aut-
self

bi-
two

con-, col-, com-, cor-
with, together

contra-
against

de-
reverse, remove, reduce

di-
separation, twoness

dis-, dif-
absence; opposite;
reverse, remove

ex-, ef-, e-
out of, from

in-, im-
in

in-, im-, il-, ir-
not

inter-
between, among

intra-
inside, within

intro-
in, inward

mis-
wrongly, badly

mono-, mon-
one, alone

multi-
much, many

ob-, oc-, of-, op-
toward, against

per-
through, thoroughly

poly-
much, many

post-
after, later; behind

pre-
before

pro-
forth, forward

re-
back, again, anew

sub-, sup-, suc-, suf-
under; lesser

super-, sur-
superior, above; additional

trans-
across

tri-
three

un-
not, opposite of;
reverse an action

uni-
one

Suffixes

-able
able to, capable of, liable to

-age
action or result of an action;
collection; state

-al
relating to, characterized by

-ance, -ancy
state or quality of; action

-ant
inclined to; being in a
state of; someone who

-ate
cause, make; state, condition;
someone who

-en
made of; cause to be or have;
become

-ence, -ency
state or quality of; action

-ent
inclined to; being in a state of;
someone who

-er
more

-er, -or
someone who; something that

-ery, -ary, -ory, -ry
place where; collection,
condition, or practice of

-est
most

-ful
full of

-hood
state, quality, or condition of

-ial
relating to, characterized by

-ian
person who; of, relating to,
belonging to

-ible
able to, capable of, liable to

-ic
relating to, characterized by

-ice

state or quality of

-ine

of, pertaining to; chemical
substance

-ion

act, result, state of

-ious

full of, characterized by

-ism

act, condition, doctrine, or
practice of

-ist

someone who

-ite

quality of; follower or resident
of; mineral product

-ive

performing or tending toward
an action

-ize

cause to be or become

-less

without, lacking

-ly

in the manner of

-ment

state, act, or process of

-ness

state, quality, or
condition of

-ous

full of, characterized by

-ship

state, quality, or
condition of; skill

-ty, -ity

state or quality of

-ure

act, process; function or body
performing a function

-ward

direction

-y

characterized by

From Tim Brown and Deborah F. Knight, *Structures in Spelling,* New Readers Press, 1990, pp. 158, 160.